Spike Milligan was born at A̶ in 1918. He received his first education in ̶ ̶ ̶ ̶ Hyderabad Sindh desert and graduated from there ̶ ̶ ̶ ugh a series of Roman Catholic schools in India and England, to the Lewisham Polytechnic. Always something of a playboy, he then plunged into the world of Show Business, seduced by his first stage appearance, at the age of eight, in the nativity play of his Poona convent school. He began his career as a band musician but has since become famous as a humorous script-writer and actor in both films and broadcasting. He was one of the main figures in and behind the infamous Goon Show. Among the films he has appeared in are *Suspect*, *Invasion*, *Postman's Knock*, *Milligan at Large* and *The Three Musketeers*.

Spike Milligan's published work includes *The Little Potboiler*, *Silly Verse for Kids*, *Dustbin of Milligan*, *A Book of Bits*, *The Bed-Sitting Room* (a play), *The Bald Twit Lion*, *A Book of Milliganimals*, *Puckoon*, *Small Dreams of a Scorpion*, *The Mirror Running* (a book of poetry), *Transports of Delight*, *The Milligan Book of Records*, *Games, Cartoons and Commercials*, *Badjelly the Witch*, *Dip the Puppy*, *The Spike Milligan Letters* and *More Spike Milligan Letters*, both edited by Norma Farnes, *Open Heart University*, *The Q Annual*, *Unspun Socks from a Chicken's Laundry*, *The 101 Best and Only Limericks of Spike Milligan*, *There's a Lot of It About*, *The Melting Pot*, *Further Transports of Delight*, *Startling Verse for All the Family*, *The Looney: An Irish Fantasy*, *The Lost Goon Shows*, *It Ends With Magic* and *The Bible, According to Spike Milligan*. With Jack Hobbs, he has also written *William McGonagall: The Truth at Last*, *William McGonagall Meets George Gershwin* and *William McGonagall – Freefall*.

His unique and incomparable seven volumes of war memoirs are: *Adolf Hitler: My Part in His Downfall*, *'Rommel?' 'Gunner Who?'*, *Monty: His Part in My Victory*, *Mussolini: His Part in My Downfall*, *Where Have All the Bullets Gone?*, *Goodbye, Soldier* and *Peace Work*. To celebrate his seventieth birthday Penguin published a special edition of his first novel *Puckoon*. Spike Milligan received an honorary CBE in 1992.

LADY CHATTERLEY'S LOVER

ACCORDING TO SPIKE MILLIGAN

PENGUIN BOOKS

Thanks are due to
the Estate of Frieda Lawrence Ravagli

PENGUIN BOOKS

Published by the Penguin Group
Penguin Books Ltd, 27 Wrights Lane, London W8 5TZ, England
Penguin Books USA Inc., 375 Hudson Street, New York, New York 10014, USA
Penguin Books Australia Ltd, Ringwood, Victoria, Australia
Penguin Books Canada Ltd, 10 Alcorn Avenue, Toronto, Ontario, Canada M4V 3B2
Penguin Books (NZ) Ltd, 182–190 Wairau Road, Auckland 10, New Zealand

Penguin Books Ltd, Registered Offices: Harmondsworth, Middlesex, England

First published by Michael Joseph 1994
Published in Penguin Books 1995
5 7 9 10 8 6 4

LADY CHATTERLEY'S LOVER

ACCORDING TO SPIKE MILLIGAN

ONE

OURS IS essentially a tragic age. There's Barbara Cartland, John Major, etc. But we have got to live no matter how many skies have fallen. Horizontal, this was Lady Chatterley's position in society: she spent long periods like it, looking up. However, she married Clifford Chatterley in the upright position. They had a month's honeymoon in a bed in Lewisham. Then came the war. Soon he was shipped to France to the Front. Alas, he suffered a direct hit by a German 155mm shell, his bits were shipped back to England in a paper bag and handed to Lewisham General Hospital. As they were, a groan came from the bag, 'No! Not Lewisham,' it said. His hold on life was tenacious. He didn't die. The doctors lay all his bits out on a table – and, like a jigsaw, put him together. The fact that he had six fingers on one hand, four toes and a finger on the other was by the way, and when he coughed it came through his ear. The doctors pronounced him better but, alas, from the waist down he was paralysed for ever with a dead willy.

Clifford and Constance made home in Wragby Hall, the family seat, there was also a family table and family wardrobe. Clifford's father had been killed in the Boer War during the siege of Ladysmith. He was hiding in the NAAFI when a tea urn fell on his head. Clifford was now a Baronet, Constance was Lady Chatterley. To keep up tradition they dressed for dinner and undressed for bed. Lady Chatterley now knew about Lord Chatterley's dead willy; at unexpected moments she found herself singing, 'Close the shutters, willy's dead.' It preyed on her mind, but more on her body. They started housekeeping on the three pounds his father had left them in his will. They had to scrimp, every day they were scrimping, by the end of a week of scrimping Lady Chatterley was exhausted.

Clifford had a sister, but she had departed, that is, she caught the ten-twenty from Victoria and was never seen again. He had an elder brother but he had been killed in the War: a tea urn fell on his head. Crippled for ever, with a dead willy, and knowing he could never have children, he was not really downcast – pissed-off, yes – but not downcast. He could wheel himself about in a wheelchair and whistle 'The Trout' by Schubert. Having suffered so much, even now he could hear his wife scrimping in the kitchen; he remained cheerful, very chirpy: he liked imitating bird songs. 'Cuckoo, cuckoo,' he'd go. His shoulders were broad, his hands were strong, his nose was strong, even his ears were strong. He was expensively dressed, a cloak of scarlet velvet trimmed with ermine and a gold crown; hidden were underpants from Marks and Spencer's – what he had to put in them wasn't much.

Lady Chatterley was a ruddy country-looking girl with soft brown hair, a sturdy body (big tits). She was full of unusual[1] energy, that is, without any warning she would tuck her skirt into her bloomers, then taking up a sprinter's start position, shout bang!, then race out the back door to return hours later, exhausted. She had big wonderful eyes. By her demeanour she seemed to come from a village; not so, she came from East Ham. Her father was Sir Malcolm Reid, once a well known RA but only once. Her mother was a cultivated woman – she was born in a greenhouse,

---

[1] Not quite sure what this means. Ed.

brought up in France and brought down in London; she joined the Fabians with people like Bernard Shaw. It was amazing, in her lodge there were eighteen people who looked like Bernard Shaw, while Bernard Shaw didn't look like anybody else.

Lady Chatterley had had what might be called an aesthetic upbringing, taken to Paris, Florence, Rome to breathe in art; she breathed in ten Leonardo da Vincis, six Van Goghs and three van drivers, then she was taken in another direction roughly NorNorEast, to The Hague and Berlin to great National Socialist conventions, to hear Adolph Schitz sing 'The Trout' in fluent German. She and her sister, therefore, were never daunted by art or politics: attending a political rally they would shout at the speaker, 'We are not daunted.' The same at the National Gallery seeing a painting by Turner, Constance said quite loudly, 'Turner doesn't daunt me.' They had been sent to Dresden for music, among other things, like the pole-vault, arm-wrestling and weaving. They had a good time there, they often pointed to a bed and said, 'I had a good time there.' They mixed freely with Cherman students, members of the Hitler Jungen; they argued with them, among other things like pole-vaulting, arm-wrestling and weaving. They tramped off to the Black Forest, and the brown and grey forests with sturdy thigh-slapping youths playing guitars and screwing, they sang the Wandervogel songs and screwed. It was freedom. Free! that was the word. Screwing! that was another word. Out in the open world, out in the forests of the morning and with lusty and splendid-throated[2] fellows free to do as they liked, pole-vaulting, arm-wrestling, weaving, river-drinking, fucking, and free to *say* what they like, and what they liked voz 'zer fuckink'. It was the talk that mattered; the impassioned interchange of talk.

[2] Fellows with splendid throats.

ADOLPH: 'Vould you like ein fuck darlink?'

CONSTANCE: 'Oh, what wonderful interchange
               of talk.'

Love was only a minor accompaniment, as was banjo-playing in coitus. Constance and her sister had had their tentative love affairs: by the time they were eighteen they had tentatively screwed themselves silly with the young men with whom they talked so passionately and sang so lustily in freedom, and who wanted of course *the love connection*, that is, ein shag. The girls were doubtful (eh?) but then the thing was so much talked about, like have you seen Hans's thing? It's bigger than Helmut's. And the men were *so* humble and *craving*, they would crawl on their knees before passing women, pleading 'Please Fraulein, just von more shag.' They even tried to bribe women into it with gifts of apple strudel, frogs' legs and camel rides. But oh dear, why couldn't a girl be queenly, and give the gift of[3] herself? Over to you dear reader. So they *had* given the gift of themselves to the Chermans with whom they had the subtle arguments. It was quite easy you just lie down and open your legs. The intimate arguments were usually 'Your place or mine?' The discussions were the great thing, the greatest thing was Kurt's: it was twelve inches long and on a clear day could be seen from the roof of the Reichstag.

The lovemaking and connection were only a sort of primitive reversion and a bit of an anti-climax, in fact Constance's bed was littered with bits of anti-climaxes. One was less in love with a Cherman afterwards, as if he had trespassed on one's privacy: an inner kingdom, well last night he did that, he went all over her privacy and up her inner kingdom. For, of course, being a girl, one's

[3] Shag.

whole dignity and meaning in life consisted in the achieve-
ment of an absolute, a pure and noble freedom. (How's
that?) What else but to shake off the old, and they'd done a
lot of that. And however one might sentimentalize, this sex
business was one of the most ancient, sordid connections,
from these sordid connections one could get crabs and the
clap. The poets who glorified it were mostly men.

> *In the Moonlight*
> I love you in your negligée,
> I love you in your nightie,
> But when moonlight flits across your tits
> By Christ all fucking mighty.
>
> Anon.[4]

Women have always known there was something, something *higher*, so would they be satisfied with Kilimanjaro
(19,321 feet)? Now the beautiful, pure freedom of a woman
was infinitely more wonderful than sexual love, indeed let
us go further, it was better than cod and chips, better than
No. 4 Ringstead Road, Catford SE6. Men lagged so far
behind in this matter, also in the making of Spotted Dick,
curtains and relief massage. Men insisted on the sex thing
like dogs. A woman had to yield, a man would go up to a
woman in the street, drop his trousers and say, 'Yield' then
jump on her and do it doggie-fashion (more to come
folks!).

A man was like a child with his appetites, it was fish
fingers or fucking. A woman had to yield to him when he
wanted, it became awkward in the Tube in rush hour, but
she could delay him with fish fingers. If she didn't yield he
would turn nasty and spoil a pleasant connection from the
Bakerloo to the Northern Line. But a woman can yield to
a man without yielding her inner self: while he's banging
away, she is free to read *The Times*, smoke a cigarette, or

[4] Unknown Second World War soldier.

sing popular songs. Certainly she could take him without giving herself into his power, all his power coming from the two eggs and bacon he had at breakfast and a cheese sandwich at lunch. She only had to hold herself back in intercourse (woah!) and let him finish without her, this she did by going into the next room and let him finish on his own, and then she could achieve her orgasm alone while he was merely her tool. She could use her sex thing to have power over him, all she had to do was wait for a hot night then flash her fanny at him.

The War came: the girls were hurried home, leaving behind a sea of erections. Neither was ever in love with a young man unless he and she were verbally near, and naked. 'Am I verbally near enough, mein darling?' he would say, banging away. Soon he would be serving the Kaiser, right now he was serving her.

When the girls came home on holiday in 1913, their father could see they had had the love experience, they were both in wheelchairs. *L'amour avait passé par là.*[5] But he was a man of experience, he too had experienced crabs and clap. As for mother, she was a nervous wreck, in the days of her life, she only wanted the girls to be free. 'Never charge for it,' she said. She herself had never been able to be herself, sometimes she was Marie Antoinette, sometimes Salome, other times she was the bride of Franken-stein: being herself was denied her. When she came down to breakfast her husband would say, 'Good God, not you again!' There and then to please him she turned into a werewolf, heaven knows why. She had her own income from her fruit stall at Covent Garden. She blamed her husband – at night she would shout through his bedroom key-hole, 'You are to blame.' Actually her condition was nothing to do with Sir Malcolm and his key-hole, he left his spirited greengrocer wife to 'rule the roost', and went

[5] The pen of my aunt is in the garden.

his own way — which led to Miss Whiplash in Streatham. So the girls went back to Dresden (these were the days before Bomber Harris), and their music, the university, the young men and screwing, and their lovely young Chermans with poetry on their lips. 'Ach you are still ein gute shag darlink.' O how exciting were the things the young Chermans thought, the poetry they wrote. There on the lavatory wall it was 'Connie is ein gute shag.' O the romance of it! In fact Connie's young Cherman was musical: in the middle of screwing he would leap off her and sing 'The Blue Danube' — how she loved him for it. Hilda's Cherman was mechanical, he did it with a stop-watch in his hand. 'Von two three in! Von two three Aus!' How she loved him for it!

In the sex-thrill within the body (Faster! Adolph Faster!) the sisters nearly succumbed to the strange male power, football. But the Chermans in exchange for the sex-thrill, gave each of them a year's subscription to the Volkischer Beobachter. Then one night of this sex-thrill thing, there was a bugle call, both leapt off the girls shouting 'Zer Kaiser is calling,' and were gone, leaving the girls steaming from every orifice. It was War. To avoid an attack by the Second Battalion of Prince Ruprecht's regiment, the girls fled back to England in time for their mother's funeral who, to please her husband, had died as Queen Salote of Tonga. By Christmas 1914 both the girls' Chermans were dead, both shot by jealous French husbands home early on leave, the sisters wept, they had loved their Chermans passionately, but (wait for it) underneath forgot them, where else but underneath where it all happened?

Both sisters lived in their father's Kensington house, mostly owned by the Bradford and Bingley. They 'mixed' with the young Cambridge set, flannelled fools who stood for freedom but never a round of drinks. They were 'well-bred', with an ultra-sensitive manner. Some of the men used eyeliner, if you touched one they screamed. Hilda suddenly found a flannelled fool with a big one and married him before it went down. Constance did a mild form of war work, she made mild cups of tea for wounded soldiers. She consorted with the flannelled fools from Cambridge who mocked at everything, they even mocked wheelbarrows, hat-stands, fish and Mount Everest.

Her 'friend' was Clifford Chatterley. With the war he had hurried like the clappers from Bonn, where he was studying coal-mining; he brought back a hundredweight sack of best nuts. This impressed Constance – he gave her one of the best nuts as a love token. 'Oh, Clifford, I'll burn it when I'm on my own,' she sighed. Clifford was of landed aristocratic society, he never went anywhere on horseback. Constance's class was of the well-to-do intelligentsia, who only drank Horlicks and squeezed the toothpaste tube from the bottom. Clifford, even on horseback, was frightened of the middle and lower classes and of foreigners armed with pistols, swords and bows and arrows; another thing was unattended fish tanks.

Constance fascinated him – the thought of her burning that piece of coal just for him and his horse he found very moving. Now he had become a first lieutenant in a smart regiment[6] he mocked anybody not in uniform. 'You coward,' he'd say. 'Take that civilian suit off.' Most of all he rebelled at his own class. 'You coward,' he'd say to them, 'take that civilian suit off!' Where he lived the streets were strewn with suits.

The armies were ridiculous men who, when blown up, would say 'This is ridiculous.' A man shot in, say, the leg would point to it and say, 'That is ridiculous.' On some gravestones it might say, 'Pte L. Conway, he was ridiculous.' And those ridiculous generals, red-faced Kitchener, pink-faced French, off-white Haig, all bird-brained.

[6] Very smart, they never went to France.

> He's not a bad bloke
> Said Harry to Jack
> As they humped their way forward
> With rifle and pack
> But he did for them
> With his plan of attack.[7]

Sir Geoffrey, Clifford's father, was *intensely* ridiculous, chopping down his trees, and weeding men out of his colliery to send them to the war in France. He sent them off with a hundredweight sack of coal. As the ship sailed he could hear them calling 'You bastard!' Many of them were killed by falling tea urns.

In 1916 Herbert Chatterley was killed by bronchitis, his CO wrote to Lady Chatterley, 'Your son died heroically of bronchitis for his country,' so Clifford became heir. There now was the threat of conscription: soon England was a country of men hiding in coal-cellars, cupboards, and up trees. Sir Geoffrey chopped trees to find them, dressed as a nun. Sir Geoffrey, like Lloyd George, stood for England and St George but sat for China and Sun Yat Sen. Sir Geoffrey wanted Clifford to produce an heir: 'One good shag should do it my son.' He tried it, but being on his own didn't help. No. He would have to marry.

The gay excitement had gone out of the war, so far over a thousand gays had been killed; their lipstick and eye make-up were returned to their next of kin.

The Chatterleys lived an isolated life at Wragby; they were cut off from the industrial Midlands that included Watson & Sons Steelmill, Mason & Mills Jam Factory, Rudge Witworth Bicycle Assembly-plant, the Haliwell Custard Works. These had been part of their early lives. 'What I miss most', said Clifford, holding back his tears, 'is

[7] Siegfried Sassoon.

the Jam Factory.' The three children swore they would
always live together. 'We'll bloody well live together.' But
now Herbert was dead. 'Ah!' said Sir Geoffrey cheerily.
'One down, two to go.' He put pressure on Clifford to
marry, and this he did. As Clifford lay in bed, he would
lay a barn door on him, then keep adding weights until he
succumbed. So almost pressed flat, Clifford married
Constance.

As a wedding present Lord Geoffrey gave them a tree.
The happy couple were 'as intimate as two people who
stand together on a sinking ship': on the *Titanic* they'd
have drowned! On honeymoon the sex part did not mean
much to him. He was not keen on his 'satisfaction'. No, he
was more satisfied by the memory of Mason & Mills Jam
Factory. Constance wanted children, if only to outnumber
Clifford, but, alas, early in 1918 in action in France a
NAAFI tea urn fell on his back, paralysing him from the
waist down, so there was to be no child, and Sir Geoffrey
died of chagrin – he had contracted it in Harrods: it was all
over his body.

TWO

CONSTANCE AND CLIFFORD came home to Wragby by wheelchair. Wragby was an old house begun in the eighteenth century and added to till it reached the nineteenth. From his windows could be seen the belching chimneys of Tevershall coal-mine. The village was rows of brick houses, sharp angles, wilful blank dreariness. The people who lived in them all had sharp angles and wilful blank dreariness. In Wragsby, when the wind was that way, the house was full of the stench of sulphur, some days it was the coal-mine, other times it was Clifford. At night Constance could see the glow of the furnaces against the sky. At first it filled her with horror – it was like living underground – then she got used to them. In time most people can get used to furnaces, one such person was Dick Turner of 11 Grunge Terrace, Luton, a retired haddock-stretcher. Constance had been used to Dresden and screwing Chermans, it was all so different here: all there was was Clifford's dead willy. Clifford thought this countryside had a will of its own and the people had guts. Constance wondered what else they had. Well, they had piles, varicose veins, and rheumatism. Between the village and Wragby there were no communications. Clifford tried carrier pigeons, but the villagers ate them. The villagers kept at a distance, they found one mile the best, however tradesmen lifted their caps to Lady Chatterley, revealing

mostly bald heads and dandruff. Sometimes it revealed
pork pies and other rationed goods. They nodded awk-
wardly at Clifford, they would turn their back to him,
raise one leg, pull their heads inside their shirt and shout
'Owdo' through a buttonhole. At first Lady Chatterley
suffered resentment from the villagers. She hardened herself
to it – she rubbed her body with arnica, it became a sort of
tonic, it was something to live up to. There were many
tonics one could live up to – Keplers Malt, Virol, and Dr
Hall's Invalid Wine. The villagers' social rule was 'You
stick to your side, we'll stick to ours.' What it was to stick
to your side they never said.

The villagers sympathized with the Chatterleys in the
abstract, something they were often in. In the flesh it was –
You leave me alone, so to leave somebody alone you had
to have flesh on. The miners' wives were all Methodist, a
doctor examined one and found her all Methodist from
head to foot. The way the miners' wives treated Lady
Chatterley puzzled and baffled her, it also biffled and
boffled her, the suspicious way they met her overtures,
even the whole 1812 complete with maroons and cannons
didn't impress. In all this Clifford stood his ground, not
easy from a wheelchair. The miners neither liked nor
disliked him, he was just one of those things like the pit-
bank. Try as he might, even with make-up, he failed to
look like the pit-bank. At one stage, for a fleeting moment,
he looked like Dick Turner, the haddock-stretcher, as for
being just one of those things, one of his things wasn't
working.

Clifford was self-conscious about being crippled; he
hated seeing anyone except servants, the one exception
being Dick Turner, a retired haddock-stretcher. Clifford
had to sit in a wheelchair, also a wheeled chest-of-drawers,
but most of all he liked to be wheeled around in a gas
stove: he loved variety. He always dressed well, he wore
those careful Bond Street neckties, he only ever shopped in

careful Bond Street. Constance and he were attached to each other, they used a chain. Connie stuck to him passionately, using double-sided tape. With him and people there was little or no connection, like Piccadilly to the Circle Line. He had no feelings for the miners, in all his life he had never felt one. He saw them as objects. A wash jug, a fish knife, a Ming vase, a mounted stuffed fish, a sheet anchor, an inlaid basalt snuff box, a three-piece dressing-table set and, strangely enough, a mushroom farm. The miners' life seemed as unnatural as hedgehogs'.[8]

Clifford was remote from mankind. He was not in touch, he was not in touch with anybody except Dick Turner, the haddock-stretcher. Clifford depended on Constance, he needed her every moment, with a ten-minute break every hour. Strong as he was, he was helpless. He tried shouting 'Help!' from his wheelchair but nothing happened. On holiday on the coast at Hastings he shouted out 'Help!' loudly from his window, and the Rye lifeboat put to sea to save him.

At Wragby he had a bathchair with a motor which he drove at eighty miles per hour through the village trying to kill miners. But always he was like a lost thing. To comfort him Constance let him spend the night at the railway lost property office and she claimed him in the morning. He needed Constance to assure him he existed. So she told him he existed. 'Darling, guess what? You exist!' He took it very well and spent another night at the railway lost property office.

Still he was ambitious, he wanted to be a train-driver, but a train-driver in a wheelchair would never work, the train service was bad enough. He took to writing stories. 'Once upon a time,' he started. Constance helped him with all her might. 'Yes, darling,' she said with all her might. 'That's very good, darling,' she'd say with more might. Of

[8] There is nothing unnatural about hedgehogs. Ed.

the physical life they lived, there was very little – a better description would be bugger-all. She had to supervise the house and the servants, the aged butler had served the late Sir Geoffrey for dinner, they say he tasted delicious.

In the meantime Clifford's writings became popular. So Lady Chatterley, with the aid of aged servants, ran Wragby Hall. It was in her second winter of discontent at Wragby with aged servants, that her father said: 'I hope you're not becoming a demi-vierge.'

'A demi-vierge!' she repeated, automatically putting her hand over it.

To crippled Clifford he said, 'Being a demi-vierge doesn't suit Connie.'

'Demi-vierge,' repeated Clifford as he hurriedly thumbed through the *Concise Oxford Dictionary of Useless Sexual References*. 'It means half a virgin,' he said, closing the book and setting fire to it – he was like that. 'Well, half a virgin is better than none,' he laughed. All the while Lady Chatterley's father was trying to release the brakes on Clifford's chair and push him down the stairs. 'What's wrong with only being half a virgin?' said Clifford.

'Well,' said Sir Malcolm, 'she's getting thin . . . angular, it's not her style.'

'Then whose style is it?' said Clifford.

'It's Mademoiselle Marie la Taché of 17 Rue de Lyon, Paris.'

'Oh,' said Clifford with as much meaning as possible.

'Constance is not the pilchard type of girl, she's a bonny Scotch trout,' said Sir Malcolm.

'I disagree,' said Clifford. 'She's more of a boiled hake of a girl.'

'How dare you call my daughter a boiled hake of a girl,' said Sir Malcolm, still fiddling with the brakes on Clifford's wheelchair.

'I challenge you to a duel,' said Clifford.

'Name your weapon,' said Sir Malcolm.

'I name my weapon Dick,' said Clifford.

'Very well,' said Sir Malcolm. 'It's Dicks at fifty paces.'

He wanted to say something to Constance about the demi-vierge business, like should they start one, also the half-virgin state of her affairs, was she having any? He was at one with her mind, but bodily non-existent: neither could bear to drag in the *corpus delicti*. Who wants that on the carpet when you're having dinner?

Constance guessed her father had said something to Clifford when she saw them duelling with weapons called Dick. She knew that Clifford didn't care whether she was a demi-vierge or a boiled hake of a girl. She knew that she was too thin every time she fell through the kitchen grating.

They had been two years at Wragby, Clifford writing his novels and Constance falling through the kitchen grating. She didn't feel she was leading a real life; she was a figure somebody had read about in the *Fishmongers' Gazette*, he saying she was not a pilchard girl but a boiled hake one. Her father, Sir Malcolm, had criticized Clifford's novels and said they had nothing in them. Clifford challenged him to a duel, wheelchairs at fifty paces. 'Why should there be anything in them?' said Constance. She thought 'Sufficient unto the day is the evil thereof,' also 'Wealth maketh many friends but the poor is separated from his neighbour' (*Proverbs* 9:4), 'The slothful man sayeth, there is a lion without, I shall be slain in the street.'

Many people were numbered among Clifford's friends, his favourites were numbers six, eight and twelve; they were critics, writers and haddock-stretchers and a Jewish duck-resuscitator. Constance was hostess to them all, the guests saw her as a buxom country girl with big tits, except the Jewish duck-resuscitator, he saw her as a 200-metre hurdler. When he told her, tears came into her eyes. 'Nobody ever said that to me before,' she said, controlling herself. It was moments like this she wanted to strip, but she knew how jealous Clifford would be, knowing he couldn't rise to the occasion.

His relatives treated her quite kindly; why they were treating her puzzled Constance, she wasn't ill. Their kindliness indicated a lack of fear, these people had no respect unless you frightened them a little. So at three o'clock of a morning she would burst into their bedroom screaming and covered in a luminous sheet. Alas, some of the guests were taken short in their beds so the practice stopped.

THREE

CONSTANCE WAS AWARE of a growing restlessness, it twitched her legs when she didn't want them twitched, like at the Opera. It jerked her spine, when she didn't want it jerked: on the loo, her arms shot up in the air, when she didn't want them there, at a dinner party throwing her chicken leg in the air. It thrilled inside her body.[9] She felt she must jump into water and swim away from it. She tried it in the bath but only got as far as the taps, it was a mad restlessness, what she needed was a good fuck, and she was getting thin. As a precaution Clifford put a grill over the bath plug-hole. Vaguely she knew herself that she was going to pieces, when she walked bits fell off her. Her father warned her, 'Why don't you get yourself a beau, someone to give you a good fuck?' She said she would think about with Clifford as he was, that's all she could do about it.

That winter Paddy Michaelis, an Irishman who had made money by his plays in London and New York – plays for the smart set, until they realized that, like Oscar Wilde, he made them look fools, so he was cut dead and his corpse thrown into the refuse-can – a miracle survivor, here he was, an inauspicious moment in his career, he was skint. Being asked to Wragby, he was grateful for a night's

---

[9] Lawrence doesn't say what. Ed.

lodgings. He arrived in a thirty-year-old Morris with a
'For Sale' sign in the window. Kudos! Having worked in
America, Paddy would have a lot of kudos! In fact Paddy
had brought a whole bag of it. Clifford was a coming
man, here he came to greet Paddy, but seeing him Clifford's soul recoiled.

Paddy Michaelis was wearing an Irish kilt and playing
the bagpipes! He played his way to the top of the steps.
'Dat was der war march of de O'Neils,' he said.

'Of course it was,' said Clifford.

Paddy led him to the front room with 'The brave
Fenian boys'. Poor Clifford, thought Constance, like Paddy
he wanted to be known, known to that vast amorphous
world he did not know – Cricklewood, Lewisham and
Neasden came to mind. In between bagpipe solos Clifford
was very polite to Paddy, whose halitosis reached you six
feet away. Yet this man was famous: this man, when as a
corpse, had escaped from a refuse-can and must know a
thing or two. There was something about him Constance
liked, she had caught a glimpse of it *just* hanging below his
kilt, and she caught her breath at the sight of it. He talked
to Clifford sensibly, briefly, practically, earnestly, intensely,
heatedly, ominously, paternally, optimistically, fiendishly,
hedonistically, spiritually and concluded with 'My Wild
Irish Rose' on the bagpipes. It was one in the morning
when he finished. Clifford backed his wheelchair away to
avoid the halitosis.

'When did you start to make money?' said Clifford ten
feet away.

At the mention of the word money Paddy fell in a faint
to the floor; gradually he came to. 'Money,' he said
crossing himself, taking out his wallet and kissing it.
'Money is a trick, once you make money you go on up to
a point.'

'You mean you get a head like a pencil,' said Clifford.

'Not if you're careful,' said Paddy.

There was a pause followed by a second pause, but so close together were they, you couldn't tell the difference.

Constance said, 'Is it difficult being a playwright?'

'No, there's nothing in it,' he said turning to her in a sudden flash. Again she caught sight of it and her right leg flew out.

Embarrassed she said, 'Paddy, are you alone?'

'No,' said Paddy. 'You're both here, didn't you know that?'

'I meant,' said Constance, pulling her leg back in, 'do you live alone?'

'No, I have a Greek servant. He cooks for me. I'm going to marry,' he said.

'You're going to marry your Greek servant?' said Clifford, backing away as Paddy and his halitosis advanced.

'No,' said Paddy. 'The lady of my choice, oh yes, I must marry.'

'It sounds like going to have your tonsils out,' said Constance.

'Nothing of the sort,' said Paddy. 'I said I must marry, I never said anything about tonsils, you don't have to have them out to marry. Have you had your tonsils out Lady Chatterley?'

'No,' she said.

'See?' said Paddy, 'that hasn't affected your marriage.' he said.

At dinner Paddy gave Constance long, bed-hot glances, suddenly her arm shot up, hurling her chicken leg in the air. The butler who had often played on the outfield caught the chicken leg low down. 'Owszat,' he said.

'Oh,' said Constance, 'I feel so stupid.' Clifford leant over and felt her, yes she did feel stupid.

'Don't you like chicken normally?' said Paddy.

'No, no, this chicken was perfectly normal,' she said. 'I don't know what came over me.'

'I didn't see anything come over you, you must be imagining, dear,' said Clifford.

'Please, sir,' said the butler. 'It was the chicken leg that came over.'

'Good,' he said. 'Wait there in case there are any more.'

Constance decided to change the subject. 'Do you have anybody in mind to marry, Paddy?'

'Yes,' he said. 'Mademoiselle Marie la Taché, 15 Rue de Lyon, Paris, see here.' He passed Constance a photograph.

'I don't understand,' she said. 'This is a photo of an elephant.'

'Yes,' said Paddy. 'It's very good isn't it?'

'Yes,' said Constance. 'What has it got to do with Mademoiselle Marie la Taché?'

'The elephant has nothing to do with Mademoiselle Marie la Taché,' said Paddy. 'They both live separate lives, he in Africa, she in France.'

'Don't drink any more please, Paddy,' pleaded Clifford.

'Yes, I have had rather a skinful,' said Paddy.

'Yes,' said Constance looking under the table, 'and you appear to be leaking.' In a moment of romantic weakness she said to Paddy, 'Is anything worn under the kilt?'

'I'm sorry to disappoint you Constance, but everything is in working order,' he said.

After dinner Paddy entertained them with more bagpipe music. Clifford was very moved by it, in fact he moved to another room. As Paddy climbed the stairs to bed, Constance caught a glimpse up the kilt and realized how lucky Mademoiselle Marie la Taché was going to be.

Next morning Paddy suffered a severe attack of face, looking in the mirror he screamed, 'How dare you?' My God he thought his face was falling off. He put a cushion down to break its fall. Breakfast was served in the bedroom. He told the butler to bring him two three-minute eggs, the chef computed them, sent him back one six-minute one along with a sixty-minute piece of toast.

'How would you like your coffee?' said the doddering butler.

'Today,' said Paddy. He now wondered what he should do and he decided it should be Lady Chatterley. He sent a servant asking: 'Could he be of service?' She ordered two three-minute eggs and toast and would he join her? He followed an aged manservant up the stairs, it took three hours.

Paddy and Constance sat opposite each other by the fire, unbeknown to them the aged manservant lay dead on the landing.

'Why are you such a lonely bird?' she said crossing and uncrossing her legs, easing tension in the nethers.

'Some birds *are* that way,' he said pointing in that direction. 'I know a duck who lived alone on a pond for twelve years,' he said.

'Why are you telling me this?' she said.

He stood, then racked with emotion he said, 'I had to tell someone. One day I will tell Mademoiselle Marie la Taché.'

'Oh come,' she said, 'there's no need to get so upset over a duck.'

'Ah,' he said. 'But that duck was Irish.'

'What is the difference between an English duck and an Irish duck?' she said.

He gave a wry smile. 'There is no difference, both two legs are the same,' he said. He gave her a long penetrating glance and that was that. 'Look here,' he said. 'What about yourself?'

So she looked there and said, 'What about my self?'

'Well,' he said. 'You too are a lonely bird with big tits.' At the same time (wait for it) the infant crying in the night was crying out of his breast to her in a way that affected her womb.[10]

He was a curious lover, before starting, he did a high-

[10] Classic D. H. Lawrence dialogue. It meant they wanted a shag.

stepping Irish jig, during which Lady Chatterley got flashes
of things to come. He knelt at her feet and put his head,
dandruff and all, into her lap. 'This is just for starters,' he
said. They had a good shag. It ended romantically when he
asked for a cheese sandwich. Suddenly his bottle went.

'Here, you won't tell Clifford, will you?' he said.

'No, I won't tell him simply because you weren't that
good.'

Paddy crossed himself, why not? Constance had found
him a trembling lover who shuddered when he orgasmed,
causing his socks to slide down to his ankles. He did it so
quickly by the time he finished her boiled eggs and toast
were still warm.

She said, 'Oh, Paddy darling, I'm lost!'

'Oh?' he said. 'Where did you want to get to?' He kissed
her hand and said, 'I'm going to Sheffield for lunch,' and
went. He returned briefly to tell her there was a dead
butler on the landing.

'I don't think I can stand that Irishman,' said Clifford at
lunch.

'Where can't you stand him?' said Constance. 'I mean
we've all got to stand somewhere.'

Clifford was chewing a tough steak. 'I've known cows
hurt worse than this and live,' he said.

Reflectively she said, 'The Irish have something.'

'Yes,' said Clifford. 'Alcoholism.'

She changed the subject, she told him Grundly the
butler had died on the landing.

'Oh, that is bad news,' Clifford said sadly.

'Only for him,' said Constance.

Paddy came back towards teatime. He brought back
handfuls of violets and lilies and two tins of Canadian
grade three salmon.

'Oh, what lovely flowers and grade three salmon, I must
put the flowers in water and put the salmon in the cat.'

That night he crept into her bedroom. 'I've got a hard-on,' he whispered, 'so I thought I'd come and see you.' With an animal scream she ripped her clothes off, leaving only the elastic marks from her bloomers. Lying her on the bed he took a running jump, but he bent it on the end of the bed; however, she kissed it better. He aroused in her a craving, she kept him inside her when his crisis was over – it was a worse crisis than the miners' strike at Carmarthen. And he was generous: he always left a pound note under her pillow; how she treasured it. For a long time he stayed firm inside, a firm nearly as big as Harrods.

When he finished she said, 'Oh darling, I feel lost.' So he showed her a map of the district and her exact location on it.

He stayed at Wragby three days, a sexual wreck. Clifford, blissfully ignorant; in the top ten cuckolded husbands he must have been number one. Paddy left Wragby when the Vaseline ran out. As a goodbye present he shook hands with Clifford. Earlier he had said goodbye to Constance by squeezing her tits, she fainted with ecstasy so he sat smoking till she came round with ecstasy.

'Oh,' she murmured. 'Where am I?'

Again he showed her the map and their location. When he left Wragby his foreskin was almost worn away.

Constance never really understood him; in her way she loved him, that is, lying down. By the time he left she'd almost forgotten how to stand. In anticipation of his return she bought a hundredweight of condoms. Before he left he had said to her *Une immense espérance à traversé la terre.*[11] To prepare for his return she practised undressing, getting it down to thirty seconds. She still wanted the sexual thrill she got with him by her own activity, like hockey, netball, croquet and bending over. And still he wanted to give it to her, which was enough to keep them connected.[12] She wrote to

[11] The pen of my aunt is in the garden.
[12] Original D. H. Lawrence line. Ed.

him saying how much she missed his pound notes under her pillow. Could he send one as a token of his love? She put it into her Barclay's high interest account.

After all her fornication she was terrifically cheerful. She used all her sexually aroused cheerfulness to stimulate poor crippled Clifford so that he would write at his best, she played Debussy's 'En Bateau' on the piano, she did Isadora Duncan dances. She made him happy in his own blind way, he really reaped the fruits of the sensual satisfaction she got out of Paddy's male passivity erect inside her, and there was Clifford who knew, despite Debussy's 'En Bateau' and Isadora Duncan's dances, he could never do it. But those days of cheerfulness came to an end as the glow of her fucking faded; Paddy had gone and the money had stopped coming.

FOUR

AFTER HER AFFAIR with Paddy, other men meant nothing to her, Tom Loon meant nothing to her nor did Dick Squats, Len Lighthower, nor Lord Louis Mountbatten nor Eric Grins, not even Houdini! No, she was married to Clifford, she would stand by him, something he couldn't do for her. She wanted a good deal from life but this poor cuckolded cripple couldn't give it to her, he had tried but it gave him a nose-bleed. She had insured his legs in the event of him walking again. She thought of Paddy and knew that their affair was at an end, she knew he couldn't keep anything up (Eh?). The world was full of possibilities. There was lots of fish in the sea but no chips. The vast masses of fish were mackerel or herring, so reasoned Constance, if you're not mackerel or herring, you're not likely to find good fish in the sea. Mackerel was an excellent fish and a fine swimmer, it was splendid eating, people eating it looked splendid, they were best grilled with basil, it was best to catch them already cooked, if you caught chips with them even better. So reasoned Constance.

Clifford was making strides[13] into fame, even money. He had his wheelchair resprayed, centrally heated and fitted with a periscope. People came to see him: Dick

[13] Lawrence's unfortunate choice of word for a cripple. Ed.

Squats, Len Lighthower, Lord Louis Mountbatten and Eric
Grins. He saw them all through his periscope.

Constance always had somebody at Wragby. There were
a few regular men, Brigadier Tommy Dukes who was a
regular man, there was Charles May who had constantly
been a regular man, there was Hammond who was ever so
regular a man, all intellectuals and philosophers, they believed it was 'all in the mind,' no one asks how long
someone was going to be in the WC, it wasn't interesting
to anyone but the person in the WC. 'The sex problem,'
said Hammond, tall and thin, with a wife and two children,
and who reeked of Horlicks: 'There's no point to it. We
don't want to follow a man into the WC. So why should
we want to follow a man into bed with a woman?'

'To have a look,' said Constance.

'No, no, no,' said Hammond angrily, it was way past his
Horlicks' time.

'But', said May, who was a Catholic, wore his underpants back to front to avoid temptation, 'supposing another
man started to make love to your wife, what would you do?'

'I should get between them,' said Hammond. 'I would
tell the bounder to leave and give him a biff.'

'Wait a minute,' said Charles May. They all waited a
minute, nothing much happened so he continued. 'Why
shouldn't we be free to make love to any woman who
inclines us that way?'

'Oh, be as promiscuous as rabbits,' said Hammond from
the I-am-shocked position.

'Why not?' said May. 'What's wrong with rabbits?'

'Mixamatosis,' said Hammond, pursing his lips like a
chicken's bum.

'But we're not rabbits,' intervened Clifford.

'I know that,' said May. 'Anyone can see we're not
rabbits.' He had never seen a rabbit in a wheelchair, May
reflected. 'If you want to go on you can say we're also not
elephants,' said May.

Constance was standing with her back to the fire, warming it. 'Life is a juxtaposition of appetites, nutritional and sexual,' she said.

'Not it!' shouted May. 'I don't over-eat myself and I don't over-fuck myself.'

How, thought Constance, does he fuck himself, he must be an acrobat?

'Ah, Charles,' said Dukes, 'Sex is just another form of talk. We exchange emotions with women as we do ideas about the weather.'

'Are you suggesting', said May, 'that while we're fucking a woman we give her the weather report?'

'I think', said Dukes, 'if you have emotion or sympathy with a woman you should sleep with her.'

May laughed loud jettisoning little spit balls into the air and down to the carpet. Everybody watched as they floated down. The dirty bugger, thought Constance.

'Sleep with a woman,' repeated May. 'You must be mad, you don't get any sleep in bed with a woman, you're at it all the time.'

'I still say', said Dukes, 'the only decent thing is to go to bed with her.'

'It's not only bed,' said May, 'some persons go to the cupboard, some do it in the bath, some do it against brick walls and some do it in doorways.'

How wonderful thought Constance.

'I don't think there's anything wrong in Charles running after women,' said Dukes.

'I don't understand,' said Clifford. 'Why does he only chase women who are running? There are plenty of them standing still.'

'Without women life would be like being chained in a kennel like a monk,' said May.

'Monk in a kennel?' said Clifford. 'Surely you mean dog.'

May laughed loud; more spit flew out. 'What I meant to

say was life would be like a dog chained in a monastery.'

'That's enough from May,' said Dukes. 'What about Hammond, you'll see he'll be a man of letters.'

Dukes was right, Hammond never stopped writing them.

'Then there's me,' said Dukes. 'I'm nothing. Just a squib.'

'I thought you were a brigadier,' said Hammond, the man of letters. 'How do I address you?'

'It's Brigadier T. Dukes, HQ Waterloo Barracks Aldershot Hampshire,' said Dukes. Turning to Clifford he said, 'Well, Clifford, what do you think of this sex thing?' Clifford and his wheelchair blushed. Embarrassed he picked up the telephone. 'Hello, who's that?' he said.

'Darling,' said Constance. 'It hasn't rung.'

'I know,' said embarrassed Clifford. 'I didn't want to wait until the last moment.' Then, regarding sex, he said, 'Myself I am *hors de combat*.[14] You see mine was shot off on the Somme, I got the DSO.'

'DSO?' queried Dukes.

'Yes,' said Clifford. 'Dick Shot Off.'

Clifford, in high emotion, spun his wheelchair around and fell out. Using block and tackle they restored him to his wheelchair. He spoke, 'Love between man and woman is a great thing.'

Constance's heart beat as she recalled Paddy's great thing. Silence fell. Fortunately it landed outside. The men smoked while Constance steamed. She had been at so many of these evenings, the men talk, talk, but they didn't seem to get anywhere, not even Lewisham. None of them spoke well of her Paddy. They called him by terrible names! Mongrel *arriviste*! Uneducated bounder! Charlton Athletic! 22 Gabriel Street! The Kaiser! Spotted Dick and custard! Constance thought of Paddy and wondered what

[14] War horse.

he was doing. He was doing Madge Gibson in the doorway of 17 Peabody Buildings.

Dukes was saying he had no real talent. 'I'm merely a fellow skulking in the Army.'

'Are you skulking in the Army at the moment?' said Clifford.

'No,' said Dukes looking ashamed. 'No, you have to be in uniform to do it.'

Constance broke the silence. 'Oh, come on, Dukes, please do a little skulk for us.'

Dukes did a little skulk.

'Was that it?' said May.

'Yes,' said Dukes.

'I couldn't tell the difference,' said May disappointedly.

'That's because I wasn't in uniform, it doesn't show otherwise.'

'Wait,' said Constance, 'I noticed it, when you laid face down on the carpet and did swimming strokes I thought that *must* be a skulk.'

Dukes smiled. 'I'm glad you noticed,' he said, puffing his pipe and piping his puff.

Hammond was saying, behind our backs we all spoke badly of each other, 'Else we bust apart.' Constance prayed they wouldn't bust apart in here, she'd have to clean it up.

'Fathomless spite,' said Hammond striking a 'I'm going to say something brilliant' pose. 'Look at Socrates, in Plato, and his bunch around him!'

So they all looked at Socrates, in Plato, and his bunch around him.

'Now what?' said May.

'Socrates', continued Hammond, now standing on a chair, 'found sheer joy in pulling somebody else to bits!'

'That must be very difficult,' said May. 'I wouldn't know where to start pulling. Do you know where he did?'

'Athens,' said Hammond. 'I would prefer Buddha, quietly sitting under a bo-tree.'

'What a bore he must have been, what a pointless exercise in fertility if we all sat under bo-trees.' said May. 'In any case there aren't enough bo-trees to go around.'

'How do you know?' said Hammond. Agitatedly he thrust his hands into his trouser pockets, splitting the seam of one and releasing all his loose change down his trouser leg.

'I read it somewhere,' said May. 'I think it was Lewisham.'

'It doesn't *have* to be a bo-tree,' said Hammond, picking up his change. Twelve shillings had fallen on the carpet, seven pennies in his shoe and tuppence in his sock. 'And', he continued, 'there was Jesus peacefully preaching to his disciples.'

'Why wasn't *he* sitting under a bo-tree?' said May.

'Because', said Hammond now in a fury, 'they don't grow in Palestine!' Pausing for breath he went on: 'No, we are rooted in spite and envy. Ye shall know the tree by its fruit.'

'What's the fruit of the bo-tree?' persisted May.

'It has no fruit,' said Hammond.

'No bos?' chuckled May.

'I don't agree with you, Hammond,' said Clifford running his wheelchair forward.

'Ow, Christ!' yelled Dukes.

'What's wrong?' said Clifford.

'You've run over my bloody foot,' howled Dukes.

Clifford told Hammond, 'I don't think we are as spiteful as you say.'

'Oh, my bloody foot,' said Dukes, hopping round the room, out the door, along the passage, out into the garden, through a gate and across a ploughed field and back. 'Ah,' he said, 'there's nothing like a ploughed field to cure a crushed foot. By the by when I was away was there any mail for me?'

Hammond was in full flow. 'I infinitely prefer spite to the concocted sugaries.'

'I'm not allowed concocted sugaries,' said Dukes, 'I'm a diabetic.'

'Real knowledge', said Hammond, 'comes out of the whole corpus, out of your belly and your penis.'

'Well,' said May, 'I can't speak for others but I never had any real knowledge come out of my prick, though I've listened very closely.'

'Perhaps you've got a stupid prick,' said Hammond, laughing fit to burst. 'Oh dear, I could do with a drink,' he said. Constance took him to a tap.

'Hammond thinks we should lead a mental life,' said Clifford, who thought Hammond *was* mental.

Hammond continued. 'Life is like an apple tree.'

'Why is life like an apple tree?' said May.

'How should I know?' said Hammond, blowing his nose in a paper handkerchief and going through it. 'If', said Hammond cleaning up the mess, 'if you've got nothing in life but the mental life, you are a plucked apple.'

'Well then,' said Dukes, 'we're *all* plucked apples.'

'Yes,' said May. 'I'm a Granny Smith.'

'Get plucked,' said Dukes.

A new guest had joined the party, a Mr Berry. 'What do you all think of Bolshevism?' he said as everything led up to it.

Clifford asked among them all, then said, 'I've just asked and none of us ever think of Bolshevism, why?'

'Bolshevism', said May, 'is a hatred of things called bourgeois.'

'What *things* do you call bourgeois?' said Clifford, oiling his wheelchair. 'Would you call a wooden leg bourgeois?'

'If it was on a sailor, no, but if the Queen had one, yes,' said Dukes, who sprang to attention when he mentioned the Queen. 'Here', he said, 'is a photograph of her.'

Clifford took the photograph. 'This isn't the Queen,' he said. 'This is a photograph of a horse.'

'Yes,' said Dukes. 'I haven't got one of the Queen.'

'I don't think the Queen with a wooden leg is bourgeois,' said Hammond. 'I'd say she was aristocracy.'

'Ah yes,' said May. '*She* is aristocracy but her wooden leg is bourgeois.'

'To be a Communist', said Hammond, 'you must submerge yourself in the greater thing.'

At the mention of the 'greater thing' Constance thought of Paddy and his.

'The only time I submerged myself was at Lewisham municipal baths, does that make me a Communist?' said May laughing.

'Russian Communism is nothing to be laughed at,' said Clifford.

'Oh, I'm sure they can't hear me from here,' said May.

'I can think of nothing worse than being a Bolshevik,' said Hammond.

'Yes, you could be Tom Loon, Dick Squats, Len Lighthower, Lord Mountbatten or Eric Grins, any of those,' said Clifford.

Mr Berry changed the direction of the argument to NorNorEast, roughly parallel with the London and North Eastern line to King's Cross where, in fact, at this moment the eleven-fifty train was arriving. By coincidence the engine-driver's name was Dick Squats.

'Do you believe in love?' Berry said.

'Oh,' said Dukes. 'You mean fellows fucking jazz girls with small-boy buttocks, like two collar-studs.'

There was a baffled silence, then Clifford said, 'What *are* you talking about?'

'I think', said Dukes, 'I'm talking about twelve words a minute, the world record is twenty-three held by Arthur Mince Junior, a Canadian haddock-stretcher.'

'Don't you believe in anything?' said Berry. 'I believe in a good heart and a chirpy penis.' A good penis roused his head and said, 'How do you do!'

'Renoir said he painted his pictures with his penis. I wish I could do something with mine,' concluded Dukes.

'Why not tie a brush to it and start painting?' said May.

That night Constance looked at her behind in the mirror. At no stretch of the imagination did it look like two collar-studs. What utter rubbish they had been talking, she would rather have talked to Dick Squats. Alas! He was on the footplate of the eleven-fifty to King's Cross.

FIVE

ONE MORNING Clifford and Constance went to cross the park to the woods, he in his motorized wheelchair doing fifty miles an hour with Constance running behind trying to keep up. The air smelt sulphurous, it could have been the factory, then again it could have been Clifford. 'Sorry,' he finally admitted. For the last mile Constance had hung on to the back of the wheelchair and been dragged along. When he stopped she was a mass of mud and leaves. In the wood everything was motionless, trees couldn't do much else. A jay called harshly.

'Look, Clifford,' she said, 'There's a jay called Harshly.'

But there was no game, no pheasants, quail or elephants. They had been killed off during the War, when the Germans had overrun the British lines. Clifford loved the old Oaks (*Quercus robur*) he also loved old Walnut trees (*Juglans regia*) and Rowan (*Sorbus aucuparia*). His wheelchair chugged up a slope stopping by a sapling (*Betula pubescens*). The area had been logged, patches of blackness were where woodsmen had burnt rubbish, that or coloured illegal immigrants were hiding. It was a good hiding place, when caught they all got a good hiding. Clifford sat admiring the view, the coal-mine, the slag heaps, the gasometer and the Jam Factory. Affectionately he patted a tree trunk[15] (*Aesculus hippocastanum*).

[15] Horse chestnut.

'This,' he said, 'this really is the heart of England.'
Constance thought otherwise: to her it was the arsehole.
The eleven-o'clock hooter sounded from Stacks Colliery.
Clifford beamed, 'Three generations of Chatterleys have
heard that sound.'

'How exciting,' said Constance.

Clifford looked into the near distance, say a half a mile.
His face was inscrutable; once or twice he turned and gave
Constance an intense scrute. 'This is our horrortige,' he
said. 'No, that can't be right. *Heritage*, that's it, and we
must preserve it like, like', he struggled for the word, '. . .
like the blackcurrant.' That was it! Blackcurrant preserve,
yes *that's* how he'd protect his horrortige, with blackcurrant
preserve! There was a sad pause. 'I think I'll have another
one,' said Clifford and went straight into a sad pause, to
accompany it he sang 'The Last Rose of Summer'. 'These
trees are older than my family,' he said.

'And taller,' said Constance.

He suddenly said, 'I would like a son.' With his dead
willy Constance knew it was impossible. 'It would be a
good thing if you had a child by another man. How about
Dick Squats?'

'But Dick Squats is a full-time engine-driver and has a
tight schedule.'

'He could do it between arrivals and departures.'

'No,' said Constance, 'I'd get covered in coal dust and
smell of engine oil and end up at Crewe.'

'Oh then, somebody else, you had that lover in Germany, he's forgotten now! Where are the snows of
yesteryear?'

Constance thought hard. 'I'm sorry, darling, I've no idea
where the snows of yesteryear are.'

'I wouldn't mind what man's child you had,' said Clifford revving the engine of his wheelchair till he was
obscured in a cloud of carbon-monoxide smoke.

In the cloud she could hear him swearing and coughing,

when it cleared she said, 'Having a son by another man, women have different feelings about the wrong sort of fellow.'

'Well, you ought to know, you must have felt a few in your time,' he said with a twisted grin that went round the back of his head and back again. 'I mean the man has to be intelligent, someone from Lloyds of London.'

'Would one of the Names do?' she said.

'Yes, as long as it wasn't Shaka Zulu.'

She was watching a brown spaniel, running from a tree he had been drenching. It started barking, whereupon a man stepped from behind the tree and kicked it up the arse. 'Now die for the King,' said the man. The dog rolled over on its back and lay still.

'Mellors!' said Clifford; the man saluted and came to attention. A soldier. 'Forward march,' said Clifford. 'Halt! Stand at ease! Will you turn my chair around and get it started?'

The man at once slung his rifle over his shoulder, landing it on the ground behind him.

'Constance, this is the new gamekeeper, Mellors,' said Clifford.

The man lifted his hat, showing his thick hair, he turned slowly to show it all. His hair had been shorn so severely it looked like a cross between a coconut and a hand grenade. He stared at Constance to see what she was like, she was like Lady Chatterley.

'You've been here some time, haven't you?' she said.

'Yes,' he said, 'since I kicked the dog's arse about fifteen minutes ago.'

'How do you like it?' she said.

'How do I like what, your ladyship?' he replied.

'I meant how did you like it here?' she said.

'I like it here very much, your ladyship.'

A conversation of absolute futility. Mellors went to the dog and told him he could stop dying for the King.

Starting Clifford's engine he pushed the chair to the hazel thicket (*Corylus avellana*).

'Is that all?' said Mellors, once again taking his cap off and revolving 360 degrees.

'No, you'd better come along.'

'Fuck,' said Mellors under his breath.

'No,' said Clifford, 'the engine isn't strong enough to go up the hill.'

'Neither am I,' said Mellors; for no reason he kicked his dog up the arse again.

Straining, Mellors pushed Lord Chatterley uphill till they reached a covert of Larch (*Larix decidua*). Connie ran forward to open the gate, the two men looked at her in passing.

'Eyes right!' ordered Clifford.

Mellors looked at her to see what she looked like. Yes, she still looked like Lady Chatterley and had big tits. She saw in his eyes detachment and suffering. Both were correct. The detachment was C Company Welsh Guards in which he was on the reserve, the suffering was he had piles (*Haemorrhoides vulgaris*). Mellors strained, pushing the chair, every now and then they stopped when he fainted.

'Come on, Mellors, you can do it,' said Clifford to the horizontal gamekeeper. 'Not tired, darling?' said Clifford.

'I am a bit,' said Mellors.

'I didn't mean you,' said Clifford. 'Connie.'

'No, I'm not tired,' she said, but she *was*.

Everything in her life seemed worn out, especially her fanny. It had not recovered from Paddy. Her dissatisfaction was older than the hills, about 10 million years BC. It was one of the oldest dissatisfactions in the world and had once been on view at the Kensington Natural History Museum.

They came to the house. Clifford, with powerful arms, swung himself to his house chair and fell between them.

'Ups-a-daisy,' said Constance.

'That's no bloody good,' said the cripple on the floor.

Carefully they lifted him into his wheelchair. Constance lifted his dead legs into position and just in case she counted them.

'Nothing else to go up, sir,' said Mellors. 'Ben Nevis? The Matterhorn?'

'No, nothing, thank you Mellors.' said Clifford. 'Thanks for pushing me uphill between fainting fits.'

'I hope it wasn't too heavy for you,' said Constance.

'No, your ladyship, I do have a hernia but I wear a Hollins & Gaithorpe patent truss.'

He gave Lady Chatterley an intense gaze. She gave him an intense gaze back. He then gave her in return another intense gaze. She returned it with yet a further intense gaze. Yet again he gave her a renewed intense gaze. Clifford noticed this intense gaze and gave Mellors an intense gaze for gazing at Constance intensely. Mellors took his leave, he saluted smartly, knocked his hat off, and because of it kicked his dog's arse again.

SIX

'YOUR GAMEKEEPER,' said Constance at lunch.[16] 'Where did he come from?'

'Nowhere,' said Clifford.

'And where exactly is that?' She sat elbows on the table, her head in her hands.

'Your elbow is in your soup,' he said.

'Yes, I was testing to see if it was too hot.'

'Yes, Mellors was a Tevershall boy, my father first employed him as a gamekeeper,' said Clifford.

'What does he do?' she said.

'He shoots people who trespass, poach game or dishonour the fair name of His Majesty King George V,' said Clifford, chewing on his portion of stretched haddock.

'Is he married?' said Constance.

'Was,' said Clifford, chewing on his portion of stretched haddock. 'His wife ran off with a Pakistani juggler.'

'What did she see in him?' said Constance.

'I don't think she could see in him but she knew it was curry,' said Clifford swallowing a piece of masticated stretched haddock.

Clifford looked at her with slightly bulging blue eyes. It was either his thyroid or the new jockstrap he was breaking in. There was a certain vagueness, he seemed alert in the foreground, but dazed in the background. Like a haze and

[16] Stretched haddock.

smoky mist, the haze seemed to be creeping into the foreground of his mind filling up with mist, so much so she couldn't see him across the table. When it cleared, he stared at Constance in his peculiar way, with binoculars; like a good wife she reminded him his stretched haddock was getting cold.

'Let me remind you,' she said. 'Your stretched haddock is getting cold.'

'No, it isn't,' he said, testing it with his elbow. 'It's still warm.'

So life at Wragby went on and bloody on. Clifford was sure of life and writing his stories. 'Once upon a time there were three bears . . .' Mentally he was still alert. Asleep by the fire Constance would poke him with a cattle-prod, he would spring awake and shout, 'Second Lieutenant Chatterley. C 95402A sah!' But the paralysis was spreading in his effective self. Constance felt it spread in her, it spread out the door, down the garden into the woods hard by Tiverton village and stopped just before the river. When Clifford was aroused he could talk brilliantly. Without warning Constance would arouse him, in an instance he would say brilliantly, 'The quick brown fox jumped over the lazy dogs!' Constance would pat him and give him a lump of sugar. But, thought Constance, day after day all the brilliant words seemed like dead leaves, crumpling up and turning to powder, meaning really nothing, blown away on a gust of wind. They were not the leafy words of an effective life, they were the ghosts of fallen leaves of a life of coming gloom and disaster. What a miserable cow she was.

His books were making him famous, his photograph appeared everywhere, the *Kent Messenger, Bexhill Observer*, there was a bust of him in Marks and Spencer's in Lewisham. He had an uncanny lame instinct for publicity; he would arrange to be hurled in front of an oncoming bus but pulled away at the last moment. He became one of the new young intellectuals. Where the intellect came in Constance couldn't see. (Actually it was the bathroom window.) This was the feeling that echoed and re-echoed at the bottom of Constance's soul.

'What's that noise?' said Clifford.

'It's my feelings echoing and re-echoing on the bottom of my soul,' she said.

'Well, it's keeping me awake,' he said testing his nightcap Horlicks with his elbow.

Paddy was writing a play about Clifford. Constance had heard about it long ago, 1909. Clifford was thrilled, he invited the Celtic copulator down to Wragby with Act One, what he would also bring down was the sex-act, when he arrived he gave Constance a bouquet of orchids which concealed a long-life Dutch cap. Act One was a great success, but the sex act that followed was even better. Constance was thrilled to what bit of marrow she had left. She kept it in a small snuff-box.

Next morning Paddy seemed uneasy, his hands restless in his trouser pockets, turning over the family jewels. Under his breath he counted them – one-two-three. He crept up to Constance's room and in case Clifford spotted him he disguised himself as Rudolph Valentino's Sheikh of Araby. Constance heard his knock, before he could open the door she stripped naked and lay on the bed, in one bound and a cry of 'Allah is great', he landed on her and away they went like a steam train. During this, without stopping, he said, 'Do you think Clifford liked Act One?'

Constance tried to answer but every thrust banged her head against the bed's headboard, which eventually fell off, so they started again on the carpet. It was an expensive one made in Afghanistan; it was a Fezhan made from various coloured (in this case red, cobalt blue and yellow) silk threads all knotted by hand with inlaid Muslim prayers in Arabic black calligraphy. Right now Constance's bum rested on 'There is no other god but Allah'. The carpet had been bought by Clifford's father, it had cost £12,000, and his father and mother had spent their honeymoon on it.

Still banging away, and steam coming from every orifice, he said, 'Why don't we get-grunt-grunt married?'

Constance's eyelashes fluttered. 'Oh,' she said, gradually being pushed off the carpet on to the floorboards, 'but I'm already married.'

'Oh, he wouldn't care, he's entirely wrapped up in himself.'

'Yes, he does wrap up,' said Constance, 'when it's cold.'

'I could give you good times,' said Paddy.

'What sort of good times?'

'Well,' he said for a start, 'Six-thirty, half past twelve and eleven-fifteen.' After a few more orgasms and a fag he said, 'I could give you jewels up to a point, about three pounds ten shillings; any night club like the Las Vegas at Catford; and know anybody you want to, like Dick Squats, Len Lighthower, Lord Louis Mountbatten, or Eric Grins, even Dick Turner the retired haddock-stretcher; and travel! Glasgow! Bexhill, Southend, Lewisham.' He spoke almost in a brilliancy of triumph. He had finished and it was now hanging down looking like the last turkey in the shop.[16]

'Look,' said Constance. 'It may seem to you that Clifford doesn't count. Well, he does: using his fingers he can get up to thirty.'

'And after that?' said the relentless Irishman.

'After that it would be the unknown,' said Constance.

One day Constance went for a walk in the woods. As she went, she heard voices and recoiled, crashing backwards into a tree. People! She didn't want people, she wanted a herd of Gnus, or Wildebeest as they are sometimes called. She caught a sound of something sobbing. It wasn't Gnus, or Wildebeest as they are sometimes called. Turning a corner she saw the gamekeeper and a child crying.

[16] Famous Army entertainment.

'Why is she crying?' demanded Constance, peremptory and a little breathless.

'Pardon me for saying so,' said the gamekeeper, 'but you look a bit peremptory and a little breathless.' A faint sneer came over the man's face and slid down into his socks.

'Don't cry,' said Constance to the child, at the same time in her pocket she found a sixpence[17] that Paddy had left under her pillow after his last shag. 'Don't cry,' she said to the child, giving her the sixpence. 'What made you cry?'

'That,' said the child pointing at a black cat.

'A black cat,' said Constance. 'That's supposed to be lucky.'

'Not this one,' said the gamekeeper. 'I've just shot him.'

He looked at her contemptuously, laconic, the word laconic derived from the Greek legend of the Lāocoon. Hearing this word based upon Greek legend Constance flushed, it went everywhere.

'What's your name?' she said playfully to the child.

Playfully the child said, 'Connie Mellors.'

'Oh,' said Constance. 'That's a nice name for a child called "Connie Mellors".' She turned to the gamekeeper and said, 'Is this your little girl, isn't it?'

'No,' he said. 'It's not my little girl isn't it. It's my little girl Connie.'

The little girl said, 'Can I go to my Gran's cottage?'

Constance looked at the gamekeeper, a man very much alone, and on his own . . . with a dead cat.

'Can I take her to her Gran's cottage?'

He nodded and his hat fell off and you could see he had been using Anzora haircream, the hair tonic that 'Masters the hair and costs one shilling and sixpence, and smells of lavender.'

'I see you use Anzora,' she said.

'Yes, it masters the hair,' he said.

---

[17] The price was going down.

'Can I take Connie to her Gran?' said Constance.

The gamekeeper gave a nod and saluted and smartly clicked his heels, sending shooting pains up his varicose veins. They left him to do what he had to do – kill trespassers, poachers and cats.

Constance knocked at the door, the Gran answered, she had been blackleading the stove.

'Oh,' said Constance. 'Have you been practising the black art?'

As Constance plodded home she could hear the gamekeeper banging away in the woods. If Paddy were here she too would be banging away. Clifford, dear Clifford, he still had many childish fetishes. He thought the colour green was unlucky, so to look at the lawn he wore dark glasses; he thought Jews ate babies, and bananas gave you leprosy, and you had to put on your right sock first to avoid the plague, and he ate a lot to avoid starvation. All that and a dead willy! Poor Constance. Sex, she thought. Sex and a cocktail, they both had the same effect and lasted as long, but on reflection, sex with Paddy, the cocktail would have to be in a gallon glass. A child, who's child should she have? 'Go ye into the streets of Jerusalem and see if ye find a *man*.' Oh no. She wouldn't go all that way for a fuck, there must be someone nearer, Lewisham? Catford?

One day Clifford wanted to send a message to the gamekeeper, but the messenger boy was laid up[18] with influenza. Someone always had influenza at Wragby, it was a tradition, it was believed that if nobody had influenza at Wragby, Gibraltar would fall. Clifford was worried, as that morning by mistake he had put his left sock on first and was expecting the plague; Constance set off before she caught it. In the woods, she saw nobody there, because there was nobody there. She loved the silence of the trees,

[18] That is, he was nailed against the wall.

she put her ear against a trunk and listened intently, there wasn't a sound, how do they do it? she wondered. She found the gamekeeper at the back of his cottage, stripped to the waist, ducking his head into a bowl of soapy water. He was trying to wash out the Anzora haircream that masters the hair, it had mastered his so well he couldn't get it off. Constance saw his clumsy breeches slipping down over his delicate white loins, the bones showing a little. Perfect, white, solitary nudity.

From him drifted the scent of Anzora and Sunlight soap. Turning, he saw Constance and asked her to wait inside where he joined her. The mixture of Anzora and Sunlight soap made his hair stand up like a porcupine.

'Would you care to sit down,' he said.

'No, thank you,' she said.

'Then would you care to stand,' he said, tying a pudding basin on his head to hold his hair down.

'I hope I didn't disturb you,' she said.

'I was only washing my hair,' he smiled. 'How do you like my clumsy breeches slipping down over my delicate white loins?'

'Do you live alone?' she said.

'No. I have a dog.'

'Where is he?'

'He's at the vet's having his arse repaired.'

He asked her what Lord Chatterley's ménage was. She told him, 'The quick brown fox jumped over the lazy dogs.'

'Very good, your ladyship, I'll see to that at once,' he said, giving her a twisted smile that reached his right ear and got stuck; she left him trying to straighten it out with a gurning iron.[19]

'The gamekeeper', said Constance to Clifford, 'is a curious person, he might almost be a gentleman.'

[19] Iron used to flatten out gurns.

'Is he?' said Clifford. 'Tell me when he is.'

'Isn't there something special about him?' she insisted.

'Well,' said Clifford, 'he happens to have delicate white loins.'

'How did you know that?' gasped Constance.

'I asked him and he showed me,' said Clifford finishing the last of his stretched haddock.

Mellors had been a serving soldier in India on the Northwest frontier in a war against the frontier tribes. 'He was injured in the fighting,' said Clifford.

'What happened?' said Constance.

'A NAAFI tea urn fell on him.'

'Were his delicate white loins injured?' said Constance.

SEVEN

W HEN CONSTANCE went up to her bedroom, she took all her clothes off and looked at herself naked in the huge mirror. She saw her fanny excessively hairy, looking for all the world like a crow's nest. She was supposed to have rather a good figure. She had, it was ten thousand pounds in the Halifax. Her body lacked something: big tits. Instead of ripening its firm, down-running curves, her body was flattening and going a little harsh. It was as if it had not had enough sun and warmth; it was a little greyish and sapless! And her belly had lost the fresh round gleam it had in the days of her German boy, she recalled him saying 'Ach meiner Constance! Zee your belly hast einer fresh round gleam, it must be zer fuckink!' Her thighs that used to look so quick (the hundred in eleven seconds) were now flat, slack, meaningless, the doctor had told her so.

'Lady Chatterley, I'm sorry to tell you your thighs are flat, slack and meaningless, five guineas please.' Fashionable women kept their bodies bright like delicate porcelain, and only used Fairy Liquid to wash themselves. She looked in the mirror, in profile it looked even more like a crow's nest. She was getting thinner, she put her hat on to make sure she hadn't disappeared. The longish slope of her buttocks had lost its gleam and its sense of richness. Crone! Only the German boy had loved it. Time after time he

would come up behind her, lift up her skirt, pull down
her knickers, and show his pals the slope of her buttocks
and its gleam! O what romantic days. Why oh why
couldn't Clifford lift up her skirt and pull down her
knickers like other men? Her body was shaped like 'hillocks
of sand' the Arabs say, another Arab saying was, 'Dirty
postcards, you want fuck my sister?' The front of her
body made her miserable, so she walked sideways to avoid
it.

Next morning she was up at seven to help Clifford, help
him with intimate things, taking his bed socks off before
he awoke, uncovering the parrot. Clifford had refused to
have a manservant. However the housekeeper's husband
Len helped him with any heavy lifting. For this purpose
Clifford kept two 150-pound bar bells which he made Len
lift three times a day.

'I've got to keep fit,' said Clifford.

Constance did *everything* for him, she went for walks for
him, she climbed trees for him, and when he wasn't well
ate his dinner. She swam the Channel for him, with 60,000
matchsticks she made a model of the Vatican for him, and
finally for him she won the Grand National, it wasn't easy,
she didn't have a horse. Poor Clifford, it wasn't his fault, it
was Grenadier Günter Halm in the 1041 Panzer Grenadier
Regiment who had fired the shell that wounded Clifford,
who at the time was hiding behind a NAAFI tea urn on the
Somme.

And yet was he not to blame? He was never more than
seventy-six degrees Fahrenheit. He was never warm as a
man could be to a woman, even her father was warm to
her, reaching 102 degrees Fahrenheit, but then he had
malaria, which he had caught off a NAAFI tea urn in India.
To Clifford's class you didn't show warmth, it was just
bad taste. You had to go without it, and had to hold your
own, which he frequently did, due to a weak bladder.
What was the point when even the smartest of aristocrats

had nothing of their own to hold? This was due to war wounds for many had the DSO.[20]

A sense of rebellion smouldered in Constance. What good was devoting her life to Clifford? Did he care that her thighs were once quick and were now flat? Did he care she was walking around with flat thighs?

There were people staying at the house, among them Clifford's Aunt Eva Lady Bennerly, a thin woman of fifty with a red nose, a widow, her late husband an Indian Army colonel had died in some kind of accident in a NAAFI. She was still something of a *grande dame* or a great Dane. She was a past mistress at holding her own, and holding other people's a little lower, this she did in the kneeling load position.

'You've done wonders for Clifford,' she said through lips rouged like a chicken's bum.

'Oh, I don't think it's any of my doings,' said Constance.

'It must be! It can't be anybody else's doings. I don't think you get out enough.'

'How?'

'Look at the way you're shut up.'

So Constance looked at the way she was shut up. 'Now what?' she said.

'I told Clifford', said Aunt Eva, 'that if one day you leave him, he will only have himself to thank.'

Constance wondered how Clifford would thank himself. Would he sit in a room alone and say thank you?

'Look here, my dear child,' said Aunt Eva.

So Constance looked there.

'Clifford should bring you to London — there's places like Lewisham Hippodrome and Catford Greyhound Track.'

Her ladyship lapsed into silence, smoothed by the pint

---

[20] Dick shot off.

tumbler of brandy she was drinking. Slowly she keeled forward face down on to the carpet.

'Ups-a-daisy,' said Constance, gradually Aunt Eva upped her daisies and sat down again. But Constance, still depressed by her flat thighs, didn't want to go to Lewisham Hippodrome or Catford Greyhound Track.

'But', said Aunt Eva, 'you'd be able to see Billy Bennett.'

'Is that a greyhound?' said Constance.

'No, no,' said Aunt Eve. 'He's a comedian.'

'What's a comedian doing at Catford Greyhound Track?' said Constance.

'No, he's at the Hippodrome, he's very funny, he wears evening dress and a grass skirt.'

'Would he bring the fresh round gleam back to my belly?' said Constance.

'No,' said Aunty Eva. 'He's not *that* funny.'

Tommy Dukes was at Wragby, Harry Winterslow, Jack Strangeways, his wife Olive. Winterslow owned a thriving monkey-packing factory. Those not present were Dick Squats, Len Lighthower, Lord Louis Mountbatten, Eric Grins and Houdini. The latter had been invited but was in the middle of a trick and couldn't get out. Everyone was a bit bored, there was only billiards and the pianola to dance, sometimes they just danced to the billiards.

Olive was reading a book about the future, when babies would be bred in bottles.

'It would have to be a large bottle for people to copulate in, and everybody could see you doing it,' said Dukes, who was a prat.

'It also says women should be immunized,' said Olive.

'How would you like to be immunized?' said Strangeways.

'By Rudolph Valentino on the great bed of Ware,' she laughed.

Strangeways didn't laugh, how *dare* Rudolph Valentino fuck his wife on the great bed of Ware!

'Perhaps all women will float off into space,' said Dukes, who was a prat.

Strangeways wanted children, Olive didn't, she wanted elephants.

Clifford gave a genteel cough. 'If we bred babies in bottles, all this love business might as well go,' he finished with a Gentile[21] cough that dribbled down his chin.

'No,' cried Olive. 'That might leave all the more room for fun, hide and seek, hunt the thimble and beg o' my neighbour.'

'I suppose', said Aunt Eva, draining her brandy glass, 'if fucking schtopped shomething elsche would takes its plache.' Like a great ship being launched she slowly slid face down on to the carpet.

'I know,' said Dukes. 'Morphia would take its place.' Dukes was a prat.

'So long as you can forget your body you are happy,' said the face down on the carpet.

'I never forget my body,' said Clifford. 'I take it with me wherever I go, I daren't take a bath without it.'

'Imagine if we floated like tobacco smoke,' said Dukes, who was a prat.

'I believe our schivilization ish going to collapsche,' said Aunt Eva, who already had.

'Our civilization is going down a bottomless chasm, the only bridge across the chasm will be the phallus,' said Dukes becoming an even bigger prat.

'You mean we all have to cross a phallus bridge to be saved?' said Clifford.

'Yes,' said the prat.

'I'm not walking over that at my time of life,' said Olive. 'Supposing it goes soft.'

When they'd all gone Constance felt no better, she felt herself all over but none of it felt better. Living in Wragby

[21] Christian.

was making her ill, she tried living *outside* Wragby, she got iller, bronchitis. She was getting thinner, even the house-keeper noticed it.

'Where are you mam?' she kept saying.

Every day she lay on her death bed in case it happened. She needed help. She wrote a *cri de cœur*[22] to her sister Hilda. She came quickly in her two-seater bullnosed Morris, registration EKL 482GO. She had bought it from Ward Brothers in Regents Park Road, it cost three hundred pounds, it was upholstered in tan leather. So far she had only done one thousand miles. Constance saw her coming up the drive. She ran to greet her and crashed down the front steps from top to bottom, there were thirty-two made from Portland stone.

Hilda leapt from her car. 'Constance,' she cried. 'What-ever is the matter?'

'I'll tell you what's the matter,' said Constance. 'I've just fallen down the bloody stairs!'

'Oh,' said Hilda, full of meaning.

Constance knew how little Hilda had suffered in compari-son, she would never have suffered from flat thighs. Con-stance was scraggy-looking with a thin neck that stuck out of her jumper: to show Hilda how thin she was she pulled her head inside her jumper and out again.

'My God,' thought Hilda. 'My sister's turning into a tortoise! I must stop her.' She immediately said, 'Stop turning into a tortoise! You really are ill, child!'

Hilda confronted Clifford. 'Constance is unwell and turning into a tortoise.'

'She is a little thinner,' he said. 'Where is she?'

'I'm here,' said Constance. 'Next to Hilda.'

'Good God,' said Clifford. 'You're nearly not here!'

'I'm taking her to see a doctor,' said Hilda.

'Yes, but will he be able to see *her*?' said Clifford.

[22] A cry of cur.

Next day the two sisters drove to London in a bullnosed Morris registration EKL 482GO. The doctor, Sir Ralph Fees, examined her. He noticed she had a fanny like a crow's nest. Her body lacked something: big tits. Instead of ripening its firm down-running curves, her body was flattening and going a little harsh (so far that was fifteen guineas). It was as if it had not had enough sun and warmth. 'It's a little greyish and sapless', he concluded. Then, picking up a camera, he said, 'Before you get dressed I'll just take a few pictures of you for my records.' As he clicked away he said, 'There's nothing organically wrong, but it won't do. Tell Sir Clifford he's got to bring you to town, he's got to amuse you. Tell him to buy some glove puppets, tell him to take you to Cannes or Biarritz, you've got to be amused, take the glove puppets with you.'

Constance knew Clifford would never get as far as Cannes or Biarritz in a wheelchair.

Paddy heard Constance was in town and came running, anything to save paying a taxi. When he saw her appearance he reeled back, he reeled forward and finally reeled upright.

'You're a shadow of your former self. Instead of ripening its firm down-running curves, your body is flattening and going a little harsh. Come to Nice with me, come to Sicily. I will amuse you, I've bought some glove puppets. That place Wragby would kill anybody, it killed Norris Pronk there in 1832, a tea urn fell on his head.'

But Constance's heart simply stood still, as did her kidneys, her liver and her giblets. No, she couldn't desert Clifford and his wheelchair, she had to go back to Wragby even if it had killed Norris Pronk.

Hilda talked to Clifford, who still had yellow eyeballs when they got back. Yes, Clifford was very grateful when his yellow eyeballs got back. He had to listen to all that

Hilda said and all the doctor had said.[23] Her body lacks something: big tits. Instead of ripening its firm, down-running curves, her body was flattening and going a little harsh.

'To relieve the pressure of Constance's body,' said Hilda, 'you need a manservant. Here is the address of a good one who was with an invalid patient till he died last month.'

'I don't need a manservant who died last month,' said Clifford.

'Then there is a lady, a Mrs Bolton, who will suffice.'

'I don't want to be sufficed by Mrs Bolton,' said Clifford, shaking his wheelchair in a rage.

'Then I shall telegraph Father and take Constance away, and stop shaking that wheelchair in a rage, the spokes are falling out.'

Finally Clifford agreed to be sufficed by Mrs Bolton. The sisters called on Mrs Bolton, a woman of forty-odd in a nurses' uniform seventy-odd. Hilda showed her a pound note and she immediately accepted the job. Her husband Ted had been killed in a pit disaster, something fell on his head, believed to be a tea urn. At the inquest, the coroner asked a survivor what a tea urn was doing six hundred feet underground.

'It was falling on Ted Bolton's head,' said the survivor.

Clifford got on very well with Mrs Bolton. She would say, 'Shall I do this now Sir Clifford or shall I do that?' and he should say, 'Yes, do this now and then do that.' When she finished he said, 'Come back in half an hour.' Softly she went, softly she came back. 'What do you want me to do?' she said. 'I don't want you to do anything, I just wanted you to come back. No, go away and do this and that somewhere else,' he said.

Mrs Bolton came from a very poor family. At Christmas when rich people were finding silver threepenny bits in the

[23] He said that will be fifty guineas.

puddings, Mrs Bolton's family only found pieces of paper with 'IOU threepence' on them.

Now Constance had more time to herself, she could softly play the piano to herself and sing, 'Black bottom I've got 'em'. She realized with Clifford how loose the bonds of love were; certainly they were not as secure as the nine per cent Bonds in Southern Railway her father had given her. She was glad to be alone. She could break wind without Clive saying, 'Go on, stink the house out,' and when she felt like it, she could open the window and sing quite loudly 'God Save the King'.

But she spent the evenings with him, when he liked to talk and read aloud, so much so voices from the village shouted, 'Shut that bloody noise!' When the villagers marched on the home Constance was forced to close the windows and put up the shades and hand out pieces of paper with 'IOU threepence'. Fortunately every night at ten Mrs Bolton took Clifford away to put him to bed. She did this by racing the wheelchair across the room then tipping him into the bed.

8½

T WAS A blowy day, up the legs and into the swonnicles. Mrs Bolton said, 'Why not take your swonnicles for a walk, you'll see the prettiest daffodils in a day's march.'

Constance didn't want to do a day's march to see daffodils; but on second thoughts she decided to go. After all, one could not stew in one's own juice, her mother always used Bisto. Spring was here. 'Seasons return, but not to me returns the day, or the sweet approach of Ev'n or Morn.'

'Very nice,' said Mrs Bolton wringing out Lord Chatterley's vest. 'Is it a poem or something?'

'Yes,' said Constance, who knew it was hopeless. 'Yes, it's a poem or something,' she said, crossing and uncrossing her legs for reasons only known to God (Book of Psalms, 38, iii: 'And ho they crosseth and crosseth their legs and the Lord was with them'). She was a stranger, she could walk better, she had stopped going sideways and by alternatively using first the *left*, then the *right* leg she could go forward in that order. She wanted to forget the world, and all those dreadful carrion-bodied people, Tom Loon, Dick Squats, Len Lighthower, Lord Louis Mountbatten and Eric Grins. They all had carrion bodies, most of them kept them in a refrigerator. As the March wind blew, endless phrases swept through her consciousness. 'A stitch in times saves eight.' 'You can lead a horse to water but you can't make him jump it.' 'You can't make a silk purse out of a sow's leg.' They were endless. The first wild flowers were out, as were the miners. 'The world has grown pale with thy breath.' But! It was the breath of Persephone! It had left Greece two thousand five hundred years ago and here it was at Wragby! She walked on not knowing where she was. An Ordnance Survey map would have shown her precise position on co-ordinates NE120° by SW8°. The exact spot in the woods was called Scrotts End, it was the exact spot where a woodsman called Ted Scrotts had been struck by lightning in 1831. Constance sat down with her back to a young pine tree that swayed alarmingly in the wind. There it was, powerful and rising up. It fell on her. Doing Isadora Duncan gyrations, she managed to free herself, she rose a little stiff, another little stiff was Ben Dreggs, a dwarf from Cottles Circus who died the day before.

The next day she went out again. She came across (she'd come across many times) a secret little clearing and a secret little hut made of secret rustic poles, it was where pheasants were lovingly reared and then lovingly shot. There was the gamekeeper kneeling and hammering! What a wonderful sight. She knew beneath his clumsy breeches were his delicate white loins; from him, even at this distance (100 yards) she could smell Sunlight soap and Anzora haircream. Seeing her, he straightened himself; there came the sound of agonized crackling of the rheumatism at the base of his spine. His dog started to bark at her.

'Please,' she said. 'Don't kick his arse.'

The gamekeeper looked displeased: he'd been so looking forward to it.

'I should like to sit down for a bit,' she said.

'Yes ma'am, which bit would you like?' he said, leading her into the secret little hut, and sat her in a chair by the fire. She really did not want to sit, poked in a corner by the fire though she often had been. Through the window

she watched him working, solitary and intent, like an
animal that works alone, unlike the hyena that hunts in
packs, or elephants that work in herds, or the Cape hunting
dog who also hunts in packs of up to twenty dogs. There
was something in this man that touched Constance's womb,
quite a feat considering he was ninety feet away.

'It's nice here,' she told him. 'Do you lock up the hut
when you're not here?'

'Oh no,' he said. 'You can't lock up the hut when
you're not here, you have to be here to do that.'

'Do you think I could have a key too; do you have two
keys?' she said.

'Not as ah know on, ther' isna'.'

He had lapsed into the vernacular, when he came out he
was covered in it.

'Perhaps Sir Clifford might have another,' he said.

He was out of the vernacular now, so Constance bid
him farewell and left, in the distance she could clearly hear
him kick his dog's arse.

Constance returned to Wragby to find Mrs Bolton
under the beech tree, balancing on a knoll, crouched
forward, shading her eyes. 'I wondered where the bloody
hell you were,' she said in the vernacular, seeing Constance.
With a cry of 'Ho, Hupla!' Mrs Bolton leapt from the
knoll. 'Sir Clifford is waiting for his tea,' she said.

'Why didn't you make it?' said Constance.

'Oh no . . . it's hardly my place.'

'I know it's not your place, but you could still make tea
in it.'

Constance went indoors and gave Clifford her wild
violets to smell. 'Mmm,' he said, 'sweeter than the lids of
Juno's eyes.'

Constance couldn't see any resemblance between violets
and Juno's eyelids. She told him she had been to the little
hut. 'It was so sweet,' she said.

'Yes,' he said, 'sweeter than the lids of Juno's eyes.'

She waited for his spasm to pass.

'Was Mellors there?' he said.

'Yes,' she said.

'Did he have his delicate white loins with him?' he said.

To humour him she said, 'Yes and they were sweeter than the lids of Juno's eyes.'

'Was he respectful to you?' said Clifford.

'Yes, he kept his clothes on all the time.'

'So you never saw his delicate white loins?' he said.

'No. I asked him, was there a second key to the hut, and he said there was no need, one key was all you needed to open the door, two keys were only necessary if you wanted to open the door from both sides at once, you could have a person with a third key, but then he'd have to wait until the first two had finished opening it,' she said with a note of distress in her voice.

'Was he short with you?' said Clifford.

'No, he was five foot eight,' said Constance.

'The cheeky swine,' said Clifford angrily. 'Who does he think he is?'

'He thinks he's a gamekeeper called Mellors,' said Constance.

'Oh does he! We'll soon see about that.'

So Clifford went to see about that, but it turned out to be true.

'The man *was* a gamekeeper and his name *was* Mellors. He *was* who he thought he was, but it was a near thing,' said Clifford. 'I accused him of being Dr Leo Gensberg, a Swiss brain specialist, but he wasn't having any of it.'

Clifford switched off his motor chair and took off his goggles.

'He used to be an officer in the Indian Army,' said Clifford.

'How', said Constance, 'could they make him an officer when he speaks with such a broad Derbyshire accent?'

'He doesn't,' said Clifford. 'He only does it in shits and farts.'

'You mean fits and starts,' said Constance triumphantly.

'Yes,' said Clifford. 'He was invalided out during an attack by the Mad Mullah and his Pathans, he and his battalion were charging uphill with the bayonet, he was leading them with his sword raised when he was wounded.'

'What happened?' said Constance.

'The Pathans rolled a NAAFI tea urn over him,' said Clifford.

'Why didn't you tell me this before?' said Constance with a hint of distress in her voice.

'I thought it would distress you to hear of him and his delicate white loins being run over by a NAAFI tea urn.'

Standing on one leg with one leg raised behind her she poured Clifford a cup of tea. 'Is that Earl Grey?' said Clifford.

'No,' said Constance, 'it's a cup of tea. How could you mistake it for Earl Grey? Earl Grey is in Burma on ambassadorial duty, even as I speak he is in Rangoon at the Court of King Thay Baw.'

Clifford sipped his tea. 'I tell you this *is* Earl Grey.'

It was a fine day, so Clifford took to his motor chair. He set off at forty miles an hour with Constance belting along behind to keep up.

'How different one feels when it's a fresh day,' she grasped. 'Usually one feels the air is half dead. People are killing the very air.'

Clifford looked around but could see no sign of people killing the air. 'I see no people killing the air,' he said.

'I do,' said Constance. 'The steam of so much boredom kills the air,' she gasped.

Again Clifford cast around looking for any steam of boredom rising in the area. 'I can't see any steam of boredom,' he said. 'Are you sure people steam when they're bored?'

She didn't answer because, dear reader, she was a hundred yards behind lying face down gasping for air. Clifford waited for her to catch up, all the while looking for the steam of boredom. She caught up and the chair puffed on; *en route* she gave Clifford some wild catkins.

'Thou still ravished bride of quietness,' he said.

'Ravished is a horrid word,' she said. 'Some things can't be ravished. You can't ravish a tin of sardines. And so many women are like that.'

'Like what?' said Clifford.

'Like unravished tins of sardines,' she said angrily.

'Oh, said Clifford in a puzzled voice. 'I've never seen a woman who looked like an unravished tin of sardines.'

The walk with Clifford wasn't turning out a success. She could walk, he couldn't; even then she had to run up to speeds of forty miles an hour. She wanted to be rid of him, his obsession with himself, and his own words, words like 'trulge, driick, frottle, grynculatez'.

The next day she went out again, a wet brown dog came running out towards her, he didn't bark because he'd have had his arse kicked. The man followed in a wet oilskin jacket.

'Did 'ee bark at 'eee?' he said.

'No,' said Constance.

'Oh,' disappointedly said the man, who was looking forward to kicking his arse. He saluted her without speaking. Alone he had practised saluting *and* speaking, followed by a quick saluting and not speaking. This time he chose the latter.

The smell of Anzora haircream and Sunlight soap were too much for Constance, holding her nose she began to withdraw. She walked backwards for sixty yards before she spoke to him. 'I'm just going,' she shouted.

'Yes,' he said. 'You must be nearly there,' he shouted back.

Constance nodded.

'Look,' he shouted, 'you don't have to stand back there

holding your nose. Come here and you can use this clothes peg.' She came forward and accepted the offer.

'Was yer waitin' to get in,' he asked, looking at the hut but not at her, noting that whereas the hut was bigger she was the more attractive of the two.

'Doe,' said Constance. 'I only sad a few binutes in the shelder.'

He looked a her. She looked cold. Should he light a fire under her?

'Sir Clifford 'adn't got another key then?' he asked.

'Doe, bud it doesn't batter.'

She looked at him. He looked hot, about eighty degrees Fahrenheit. Funny, *she* felt cold.

''Appen yer'd better 'ave dis key an' ah min fend for t'bods some other rud.'[24]

'Wod do you bean?' she said.

''Appen yer'd better 'ave dis key an' ah min fend for t'bods some other rud.'

She removed the clothes peg. 'I still don't know what you mean.' She hated his excess of vernacular. He had an excessive vernacular which he used at parties. 'Why don't you speak ordinary English?' she said coldly now at fifty-eight degrees Fahrenheit.

'Me! Ah thowt it wor ordinary,' he said.

The wind was blowing in a different direction so she abandoned her clothes peg on her nose and it all poured out.

'Yo got a bad cold there,' he said.

She became angry. 'I don't want your key,' she said stamping her foot on the ground, burying it up to her ankle in mud. She was tilted several degrees to the left.

''Ere let me straighten 'ee up,' he said grabbing her leg and pulling it free.

The touch of his hand on her leg sent a thrill running up

---

[24] The pen of my aunt is in the garden.

it into her bloomers up past her waist elastic where it dispersed. It was a near thing, in fact it went very near her thing. He looked at her with his wicked blue eyes, then he looked at her through his wicked brown ones.

'Why,' he began. 'Yo ladyship's welcom' ter th'ut an' th'key an' iverythink. On'y this ti'me o th'year ther's bods ter set.'

She listened to him in amazement. 'What in Christ's name are you talking about?' she said.

He pushed back his hat in an odd comic way, he had seen many odd comics do it, Ivor Cutler was one and Dirty Derick Dull, both at Lewisham Hippodrome.

'I've seen Dirty Derick Dull do that at the Lewisham Hippodrome,' said Constance.

'Well, your ladyship, if you don't want the key I'll be going,' he said completely free of the vernacular.

She went home in confusion not knowing what she thought or felt, she felt her leg where he had, but it was nowhere near as thrilling.

NEUF

ONSTANCE, EVEN though she was on Keplers Malt three times a day felt weak. In the whole world there was no help. She often opened a window and shouted help! Two or three times the fire brigade came, but nothing else. Money and sex were the two great manias. How she missed Paddy's pound under her pillow. Like Colonic Irrigation she felt washed out. Insanity, was it happening to Clifford? He had started to wear his underpants back to front in the event of the river breaking its banks! He was not aware of the great desert tracts in his consciousness, there could be camels there!

It was a lovely day. Clifford asked Mrs Bolton, 'I think I'll have those hyacinths taken away.'

'They smell beautiful,' she said.

'The scent,' he said. 'It's a little funereal.'

'I went to a little funeral,' she said. 'It was Ben Dreggs, a dwarf from Cottles Circus.'

'This circus dwarf,' said Clifford, 'what did he do?'

'He died,' she said. 'That's why they buried him.'

'What did he die from?' said Clifford.

'He died from elephant,' she said.

'Died from . . . *elephant*?' said Clifford.

'Yes, one trod on him,' she said.

She worshipped him, she did everything for him, she swam the Channel for him and was even now making a model of St Paul's out of 10,000 matchsticks.

'Will you shave yourself this morning or would you rather I did?' she said.

'Yes, I'd rather you went and shaved yourself,' he said.

Indeed, she would do anything for him, even a bank. Constance was tempted to say, 'For God's sake, don't sink into the hands of that woman.' But she found she didn't care for him enough to say it, in the long run; on a short run she found it quite easy. She had run thirty yards, then said to him, 'For God's sake, don't sink into the hands of that woman.'

'Why did you run thirty yards to tell me that? Ten would have done,' he said smiling and tapping his nose but nothing fell out.

To keep Clifford Mrs Bolton learned to type. So now Clifford could dictate a letter to her. 'C,' he would say, and she would take it down, rather slowly but correctly. Between them it took seven months to write a letter. He was very patient with her, spelling out difficult words like 'Zogxtipilxow kmtpet' and phrases in French '*Vin de Table*!'

Now Constance would sometimes plead a headache as an excuse for going up to her room after dinner, though she went there after dinner, when she got there there wasn't a sign of dinner.

No sooner had she gone than Clifford rang for Mrs Bolton. 'You rang, Sir Clifford,' she said.

'No, it was the bell,' he said.

He taught her upper-class games, piquet, bezique and knock-down-ginger. He was educating her. 'Two plus two is four,' he told her.

'Are you sure?' she said, eyes glowing with excitement and conjunctivitis.

She too was effecting him, he was becoming a little vulgar. 'Wot bleedin' orful wevver,' Lord Chatterley would say. He was becoming a little common. At a cocktail party he broke almost earsplitting wind, saying

'Share that among you!' Mrs Bolton was thrilled at knowing a man, an aristocrat, whose photo appeared in the
illustrated papers and by some terrible mistake, in the
Exchange and Mart.

Mrs Bolton worshipped Clifford, he had to stop her
genuflecting every time she came before him and burning
a candle each side of him. Under her influence he took a
new interest in the mine, every day she would bring him a
lump of coal from the day's shift. Every morning now he
would put on a miner's helmet, put coal dust on his face in
sympathy with the miners, he kept one of the mine's
canaries in his bedroom to warn of gas in the shaft, and a
parrot trained to shout 'Gas' in the event. He realized he
was the real boss of Tevershall mine, he really was the pits
(Eh?!!!). Things he had learned before the war and seemed
forgotten now came back to him: how to harden a conker,
how to cross the road and how to make a model of St
Paul's from hardened conkers. Now he sat there, his pockets
full of hardened conkers, crippled, in a tub, with the
underground manager showing him a coal seam with a
powerful torch. He said little, because there was fuck all to
say, he could have said 'Elephants' but that would confuse
the manager who would only say 'where?' and the game
would be up. He began to read technical works on coal-
mining. It was all there. 'Put canary in place then grasp
pickaxe handle by shaft, strike point in seam, remove coal,
take to surface and sell in bags.'

So *that's* how it was done! Eager for more knowledge
Clifford read the latest German mining techniques 'Put zer
canary in zer place. Grasp zer pickaxe handle und zer shaft
strike mit point in seam remove zer coal, take up zer
surface und zell in zer bags.' So the Germans weren't ahead
of us! Many new inventions were happening there! There
was one now but Clifford didn't know of it as it happened
in Brest-Litovsk. Of course the most valuable information
was kept secret as far as possible, like the company chairman

screwing the secretary. That night in his bedroom Lord Chatterley broke wind, a moment later the canary fell off its perch and died.

Clifford was interested in the technique of modern mining and canary replacement. The very stale air of the colliery was better than oxygen. Once down there he had farted, three canaries died. The mines gave him a sense of power, power *real* power, he could feel it in every skin of the banana he was peeling. He was doing something and he was *going* to do something, he did, it killed another canary. The depression was on and he wanted to pull Tevershall mine out of the hole. (How silly, most mines were down a hole!). Success as a mining boss had at last got him out of himself, he was over there. Art had not done it for him, Art[25] had only made it worse. He was not aware how much Mrs Bolton was behind him, he was always comfortable in her company, of which he was a director. With Constance he was a little stiff, it was eventually diagnosed as arthritis, in ancient Greek it was Arthron. Dr Blake told him, 'You have ancient Greek Arthron and that will be fifty drachma.'

[25] Art Blake, the family doctor.

TEN

CONNIE SPENT a good deal alone now, who set up the good deal were Twerg, Spencer and Durt Solicitors & Commissioners for Oaths. Fewer people came to Wragby, among the fewer were Dick Squats, Len Lighthower, Lord Louis Mountbatten, Eric Grins and Dick Turner, the retired haddock-stretcher. Of all of them only Lord Louis resented being a fewer person. Dick Squats had become a much fewer person as he had died. Strangely enough he died of elephant. Clifford had turned against his cronies. One good turn deserves another they say, so he turned on them a second time. He was queer.[26] He preferred the radio, usually queers prefer other men, but he preferred the radio, on it he could sometimes get Madrid or Frankfurt even London's 2LO who broadcast a talk, Musk Ox maintenance, seventy years on they wouldn't have changed much. Clifford would spend hours listening to the loud speaker bellowing forth. It amazed him and stunned Constance while deafening him, she bought him an ear trumpet but he never learned to play it. Was he really listening to it? Or was it a soporific drug he took, yes, he was on Ovaltine, he mainlined it with a hypodermic at bedtime. A kind of terror filled Constance, she fled up to her room. She had the lock changed on her door – she

---

[26] In D. H. Lawrence's day this word had a different connotation.

changed it for a goldfish. If ever Clifford broke into her room he'd have to deal with a goldfish first. He went on listening unendingly to the radio. After three months he was master of Musk Ox maintenance.

Constance was never free, for Clifford must have her there, he even marked the spot with a cross. She must be there at Wragby, otherwise he would be lost like an idiot on a moor. By coincidence at that very moment there was an idiot roaming lost on the moor, it was none other than Eric Grins who had lost his mind when, because he was a crony, Clifford had turned against him twice. Constance realized with a sense of hirror[27] how much Clifford depended on her emotionally. By using a glass tumbler against the wall she heard him with pit managers, members of the board, young scientists and was amazed at his insight into Musk Ox maintenance. He had power over what is called practical men; he was practically a man himself. The idiot lost on the moor, Eric Grins, stumbled in. Clifford lectured him, and when Eric Grins stumbled out, he was no longer an idiot but a master of Musk Ox maintenance. Clifford worshipped Constance. She was his wife, a higher being, she couldn't get higher, she was in the attic room. From it on a clear day she could see the Jam Factory, and using binoculars she could actually see the jam. All Clifford wanted was for Constance to swear, to swear not to leave him. So she swore not to leave him, 'I won't bloody well leave you,' she said.

'Clifford,' she said to him — but this was after she had the key to the hut,[28] 'would you like me to have a child one day?'

He looked at her. 'Yes,' he said. 'How about Tuesday?'

There was a long pause, it was not clear who was making it.

[27] Yes, hirror.
[28] Where the screwing was.

'Yes,' he said. 'It would be awfully nice to have a child, he could do the washing up and', he laughed, 'we could take turns at hitting him, if he didn't do it properly eh? Haw haw haw.'

What a prick he is, thought Constance, pity he hadn't got one. She listened to him with a taste of dismay, repulsion and Worcestershire Sauce, which she loved especially with steak and chips that she would eat with absolutely no sigh of dismay or repulsion. It was amazing.

That evening there were important overseas businessmen coming to dinner. Mr Umbalu Moboto, Mr Ravi Cheki-wallah, Mr Itzikazu Itchikuchi, Mr Ivanov Kurriminski. No! No! Constance would get her headache ready. Sometimes she felt she would die at this time, five-twenty and eleven seconds. By five-thirty it hadn't happened. No, it would have to be the headache. She felt she was being crushed to death (now five-forty) by weird lies like 'Your mother had marble legs' or 'The pen of my Aunt is in your garden' lies. All lies! There was nothing between Clifford and her, these days she never touched him, however, he touched her, he used a stick. He never even took her hand and held it kindly, not even her leg, no, the latter is a lie, he *did* take her leg and hold it kindly, with pliers.

THE DIRTY BITS

'I GOT YOUR key made, my lady,' he said saluting and handed her the key.

'Oh I'm so glad it's not a goldfish,' she said.

'The hut's not very tidy,' he said. 'I cleared what I could, here's the list.' He handed it to her, she read.

(1) 1 Elephant's foot umbrella stand
(2) 1 Banjo (damaged)
(3) 1 Zulu war club
(4) 1 Beckstein piano
(5) 1 Black tin trunk containing feathers
(6) 1 Ming hockey stick
(7) 1 Clockwork imitation crocodile with revolving eyes
(8) 1 Ball of string

'Oh, how wonderful,' said Constance. 'How can I thank you?'

'Well, well,' he said. 'Money comes to mind.'

She felt in her purse and gave him a threepenny piece.

Taking it he said, 'Is there any Scottish blood in your family?'

'No,' she said.

'Just asking,' he said.

He seemed kindly but distant, about a mile. A cough troubled him, he gurgled a great poached egg phlegm and gobbed it into the grass.

'You have a cough,' she said.

'Nothing – a cold. The last pneumonia left me with a cough, it's nothing!'

'How can you gob up stuff like that and say it's nothing, it's nearly a foot in diameter!' she said.

He kept his distance from her and would not come any nearer, when he did she thought she smelt burning hairs.

She went fairly often to the hut, sometimes she went oftener, that was just like often, but oftener than often. Mellors had built a shelter for the birds with five nests, when Constance came oftener again, there were five hens in it, all on the nest. For some deep reason she pined to give them something. She did, she gave them a song. 'Chick chick chick chick chicken, lay a little egg for me.' She came every day to see the chickens, she sang them 'Land of hope and glory', 'Keep the home fires burning', and 'When dat midnight Choo Choo leaves for Alabam'! Clifford's protestation at this behaviour made her go cold from head to foot.

Mrs Bolton's voice made her go cold, so when speaking to either of them she wore heavy woollen underwear and electrically heated, battery-charged boots. One day at the chicken's nest a tiny chick came prancing from the coop, a delightful little creature. Constance crouched over it with a sort of ecstasy, thinking in twelve weeks' time he'd be ready for the pot. Suddenly the gamekeeper with his delicate white loins approached.

'I came to watch the chickens,' she said.

'Do you always wear heavy woollen underwear and electrically heated boots to watch chickens?' he said.

'No, this is the first time,' she said.

Squatting beside her he unexpectedly stood up.

'That was unexpected,' she said.

Suddenly he was aware of the old flame shooting and leaping up his delicate white loins and Constance could smell burning hairs again. Tears ran down her cheeks.

'Don't cry,' he said.

'Why,' she said. 'Is the hosepipe ban still on?'

'Shall you come to the hut?' he said in a neutral[29] voice. The first signs of an erection were his fly buttons shooting off, and Constance could smell burning hairs yet again. Inside the hut he prepared the place for a shag. He took a brown army blanket and laid it on the floor, that blanket where in India[30] he had laid so many 'Bibbies', so many that some mornings before shaking it he had to break it. With a queer obedience she lay on the blanket. His foreplay consisted of putting her hand on his willy and whispering 'That's going to be all yours darlin'!' He knew how to unclothe her where he wanted but found the electrified boots an obstacle. He drew down the silk sheath of her petticoat, and having difficulty with her electrified boots said, 'Could you take these bloody things off darlin'.' Not my lady any more, 'darlin'. As Constance unlaced the boots, he smoked a fag all the while humming an impatient little tune, a tune known to many soldiers:

> There was a man who was no good
> Took a maid into a wood
> Bye Bye Black Bird
> There he took off all her clothes
> Electric boots, her drawers, her hose
> Bye Bye Black Bird
> Then he took her where no one could find her
> With a rope he tied her hands behind her
> Then he laid her on her back
> Stuck his willy up her crack
> Black Bird Bye Bye.[31]

[29] Like Switzerland.
[30] Grant Road, Bombay.
[31] Old soldier ballad.

She lay still, in a kind of sleep, with him banging away. He was doing about eight thrusts a second which was good going for a man of his years with a fifth lumbar disc problem. He stopped for a rest. She wondered why this had happened! Why was all this necessary? Was it real? Was it real? Yes! He'd started again! Finally, with a sigh he drew away from her with a loud POP! He drew her dress down over her knees, but she pulled it up to give it a chance to cool.

To signal the end he said, 'You can put your boots on again darlin'.'

In the dark she could hear him adjusting his clothing and tucking it away. He then went outside, the woods were flooded with moonlight and smelling of wild roses, he lit up a fag and farted. Constance waited till the air had cleared. It took half an hour. She went outside to join him.

'I'll go with you to the gate,' he said.

He locked the hut, put the rolled blanket under his arm and came after her.

'Are you sorry?' she said.

'In a way,' he said. 'I thought I'd done with it all. Now I've begun again.'

'Begun what?'

'Fucking,' he said.

'Fucking?' she said with a queer thrill.

'Fucking,' he said. 'There's no keeping clear of it!'

'It's just love,' she said.

'No it *isn't*, it's *fucking*!'

'You don't hate me do you?'

'Nay, nay, you're a good fuck, it was a good fuck. How was it for you?'

'Yes, for me too,' she answered untruthfully because she had not been conscious of much, even at eight thrusts a second. That was true aristocracy.

They reached the gate. 'I'll say good-bye then,' he said.

'Shall I come again?' she asked wistfully.

'Why not?' he said. 'You didn't come this time.'

He watched her walk away. He turned into the dark of the wood. He walked into a tree. He picked himself up, dusted himself down and started all over again.[32] He could see the rows of lights at Stacks Gate, the smaller lights at Tevershall pit, and screwing up his eyes, the gas lamp on the Jam Factory. How he hated jam, once contacted one couldn't escape from it, he recalled a poem by a famous poet:

> Jam, beware beware of Jam
> It will get you P.M. or A.M.
> It's always there at breakfast and tea
> That's how it gets in, you see.
> There's no escape from Jam
> It will find you wherever you am
> There's that moment of dread
> When you find it on your bread
> No matter where you are
> It will come at you from a jar
> If you can give up Jam
> You can say what a man I am.

This woman Lady Chatterley had cost him that bitter privacy of a man who had been a perfectly happy onanist. What had happened was not her fault. The fault lay there, out there, in those evil electric lights, the diabolical rattling of the mine's engines, roads roaring with traffic, that's what made them fuck! People who lived between a coal-mine and a motorway fucked themselves to death! He thought of the tenderness of her, oh, she was too nice for the tough lot she was in touch with like Ted Loon, Dick Squats, Len Lighthower, Lord Louis Mountbatten, Eric Grins and recently, Billy Bennett after a recent performance

[32] George Gershwin.

at Lewisham Hippodrome. Poor thing, she too had some of the vulnerability of the wild hyacinths, so why hadn't he fucked them? Tender, Lady Chatterley was tender, tender . . . tender where the stones under the blanket had bruised her arse, eight thrusts a second remember. He would protect her with his heart, which wouldn't offer much protection to an enraged husband approaching in a motorized wheelchair with a shot gun. He was alone, his room was clean and tidy but rather stark. It's no good, he'd *have* to buy a Bechstein. He tried to read a book about India, but tonight he found it impossible to read, mainly because he hadn't got a book about India, so he sat and thought about a book on India. He knew that conscience was chiefly fear of society, or fear of one's self. He was not afraid of himself only the sound of an approaching motorized wheelchair.

Lady Chatterley! If only she could be there with him! The desire rose again, his penis began to stir like a live bird, to make it worse it started to cluck. Putting it on the table and hitting it with a hammer brought it temporarily under control. He took his coat, his gun, the hammer and went into the night with his dog who, to avoid his arse being kicked, ran by his master, backwards. Mellors loved the intense darkness. He was rendered unconscious by a protruding branch. How he loved the darkness.

Constance, for her part, and with that part, hurried home. She would be late for dinner. She was annoyed to find the front door locked, she discovered this when she ran face on into it. Mrs Bolton opened it.

'Oh,' she said. 'There you are, your ladyship.'

It was true, there she was her ladyship.

'Sir Clifford is in the lounge with Mr Lindley, they're talking over something, it looks like a table. Should I put dinner back an hour?'

'No,' said Constance. 'put it back on the table they're talking across, they're bound to see it.'

Mr Lindley stayed to dinner, it was stretched haddock. Constance was the ideal hostess, so modest, so sensitive, so aware with big, wide, blue eyes, not a bad cover for someone who had just been screwed by the gamekeeper.

Mr Lindley was an elderly man from the north, mind you he'd have been just as old in the south. He loved stretched haddock.

'There's nowt like it,' he said and how right he was, there was nowt like it, even stretched elephant.

Shaka Zulu (1801–1847) loved stretched elephant. After eating one he said 'Umgaga xlamua daloola' (there's nowt like it).

After dinner Constance went to her room. She felt vague and confused. She didn't know what to think, if only she had a book on India. Mellors; what kind of man was he? Did he like books on India? He was kind, possibly the wrong kind.[33] He had a warm kindness, that almost opened her womb to him in another life. Was he a gynaecologist? He was a passionate man, wholesome and passionate with a big prick and a blanket. He might be the same with any woman as he had with her, I mean he had seven blankets in that hut, all very worn. But he had been a good lover,[34] he had softly stroked her loins at eight strokes to the second, and her breasts at twenty. A very good rate for a gamekeeper.

Next day she went to the wood. Ah! it was still there! But *he* was not. She only half expected him, perhaps his other half would arrive later. The pheasant chicks were running about, how lovely, it wouldn't be long before they would appear roasted on plates at Simpson's. She watched them and waited, then she waited and watched, which was exactly like watching and waiting in reverse order. Time passed with dream-like slowness. She had only half expected him, but neither half had shown. She must

[33] Traditional Ronnie Scott joke.
[34] Fuck.

get home for tea and crumpets[35] with crippled Clifford. A
fine drizzle of rain fell.

'Is it raining again?' said Clifford, seeing her shake her
hat.

'Just drizzle.'

'Drizzle? Look at you.'

So she looked at you.

'You're soaking wet,' he said.

'Yes, I was soaked in a fine drizzle of rain,' she said.

'You'll catch cold,' he said.

She was grateful for this advance prognosis. She waited
for the cold, but it didn't happen.

'Look,' she said. 'I can't wait any longer.'

She poured the tea in silence, they drank it in silence,
they swallowed it in silence, there was silence save for the
gurgling and rumbling and bubbling sounds from Lord
Chatterley's stomach.

'Is your stomach troubling you?' she said.

'No!'

'Well, it's troubling me, do stop it, put your soundproof
trousers on.'

'You never could stand the sound of tea passing through
a person. In India it's considered quite normal.'

She didn't hear him, Constance was thinking of eight
thrusts a second and perhaps an improvement on that time.

'Shall I read a book on India to you?' he said.

'No,' she said, 'I think I'll go to my room. I've got a
slight haddock.'

'You mean headache,' he said.

'No, it's a *haddock*, don't tell me what I've got,' she said.

'Very well, darling,' he said. 'Have it your way, you've
got a haddock, is it stretched?'

She didn't answer. She went to the window to dry
herself, realized her mistake then moved to the fireplace.

[35] She herself was a bad bit of crumpet. *Ibid.*

'Aren't you well, darling, can't you tell the difference between a window and a fireplace?'

'You should talk,' she said. 'You can't tell the difference between a haddock and a headache.'

Before leaving the room she said, 'Perhaps you'll have Mrs Bolton to play something with you, like hide the thimble!'

'No I'll listen in.'

'Good, then listen in to Mrs Bolton hiding the thimble.'

'No, I'll listen to 2LO Savoy Hill wireless.'

She went to her room. She heard the loudspeaker begin to bellow. An idiotic genteel voice; something about Old London Street cries like 'Stop thief . . .' She pulled on her old violet-coloured mackintosh and slipped out of the house at the side door. The fall winded her, she hadn't been as badly winded since she was a baby. She felt the rain was like a veil over the world, she wasn't where it was badly needed. The mealie crops had failed, as had half the students at London's South-east Polytechnic. But rain was falling in Burma, India and Malta so she was partially right.

The wood was silent, but in the distance Constance could hear Lord Chatterley's stomach rumbling. Yes, the wood was silent, still secret in the evening drizzle, full of the mystery of eggs and half open buds, half unsheathed flowers. The mystery of eggs had never been solved by Scotland Yard, Sexton Blake, Sherlock Holmes or Mrs Aida Blun.

There was no one at the clearing, but when she checked again she was. The chicks were all under the mother hens, one or two still pecked about, they were doubtful of themselves. Why, dear reader, should a chicken be doubtful of itself? It's not a crime to be a chicken, there is no history of a chicken committing a crime, the idea is ridiculous. So! He still had not been. She put her hands on her hips and said, 'Huh!' In time this would be a popular Hollywood acting cliché. Was he staying away on purpose? Perhaps something was wrong, perhaps he had leprosy! Perhaps she should go to his cottage, lepers need help, like catching bits as they fall.[36] No, she was born to wait. The times she'd knocked on lavatory doors and a voice inside said, 'For Christ's sake, wait.' She opened the hut door with a goldfish. Inside all was tidy, the corn in the bin, the blanket folded on the shelf. Oh, the blanket! How her heart beat. The table and chair had been put back where they'd lain. In anticipation she moved them away. Nothing made a sound, save distant Lord Chatterley's stomach. The trees, the bushes, the grass. How alive everything was. Wrong! The cemeteries were full of dead people.

Suddenly! *He* came striding into the clearing in his oilskin jacket. Thank God he hadn't got leprosy. He walked past to the coops, he squatted down.

'These chickens look very doubtful of themselves,' he said.

Constance noticed a hammer in his back pocket. 'What's that for?' she asked.

'It has its uses,' he said.

Constance, innocent of hammers, said, 'Is it to hammer things down?'

'Yes,' he nodded.

'So you've come then,' he said feeling for his hammer.

'Yes, you're late.'

'Aye, I tried not to get to the woods before the trees got here.' He paused to listen. 'What's that distant sound?'

'It's my husband.' Before she had said it the gamekeeper shot up a tree.

'Is he c-c-c-oming here?' he said.

'It's only his stomach.'

'His stomach is coming 'ere?' he said.

She calmed him, explaining the resonance of tea passing through a person at a distance. He clambered down.

'What'll folk say you coming 'ere every night?'

She looked at him at a loss, it came to thirty pounds.

[36] Ronnie Scott joke.

'Nobody knows,' she said.

'They soon will though,' he replied. 'What then?'

Again she looked at him at a loss, this time no money was involved. A burst from Lord Chatterley's stomach sent him up a tree again, she climbed up it to calm him. As she sat next to him her legs astride a branch his underpants boiled. A muffled clucking came from his delicate white loins, which he started to hit with a hammer.

'Stop,' she said. 'You'll spoil it for me!'

They climbed down, having failed to do it in the tree.

'Oh,' said Constance. 'If only you were a monkey!'

Clutching his hammer in case, he took her into the hut.

'Do you still want me?' she said closing to him. She could feel the heat in his trousers as his fly buttons shot off.

'Blastee,' he said. 'I spent all night sewing them on.'

She looked up at his averted face, but it was averted. 'How did your face get like that?'

'Like what?'

'Averted.'

'Oh, it's quite easy, you slowly move it thirty degrees to the right or left, if you moved it any more you'd be looking backwards.'

As she looked into his eyes, they were very dark, the pupils dilating and expanding rapidly, was he on something?

'Are you on something?' she said.

'Yes,' he nodded. 'I'm on two pounds thirty shillin's a week.'

Surely two pounds thirty shillings a week shouldn't affect the eyes? In the hut his eyes became accustomed to the dark, he noticed a change.

'Some bloody fool's moved the chair and table,' he said.

He bent down and kissed her unhappy face. Then, rubbing his hands gleefully, he said, 'Right,' and laid a blanket on the floor.

'I can't stay long,' she said. 'Dinner is at half past seven.'

He looked at her swiftly, 'wooshh', then his watch. 'All right,' he said. He'd have to up his eight thrusts a second to twelve. In one bound they were naked. He put his face down and rubbed his face against her belly and thighs again and again.

'Wheeee! This is fun,' he said.

She wished he would not caress her so, it was giving her a rash.

'You've got flat thighs,' he observed.

'Yes,' she said, 'but I'm building them up with Sanatogen.'

She lay there waiting, waiting, then Wallop, Bang, Crash, in he went, he was banging away, all the while looking at his luminous watch to keep up to twelve thrusts a second, he counted out loud 5–6–7–8–9–10–11–12. 'Can you go faster?' she gasped. 'I don't want to miss dinner, it's cottage pie.'

Immediately he went off at a great rate, his bum became a white blur, his thrusts gradually rode her up along and off the carpet. That and her knees began to quiver, and an old English poem came to mind. She stopped the screwing while she recited it to him:

> Knees, you've got to have knees
> They're the things that take the shock
>   when you sneeze

Without any show of appreciation, he grabbed her by the ankles, pulled her back down on the blanket and started to roger her again.

'I must go now,' she insisted. 'There's cottage pie for dinner.'

Every word came out in a jerked voice as he continued to bang away. Suddenly, to her horror, she realized he was eating a cheese sandwich.

'Just a snack,' he gasped.

'There's something sticking in me through the blanket,' she said.

'It's my fly buttons,' he said.

Then it was all over, mostly over her. 'I'll light the lamp,' he said.

So far they'd been fucking in Braille. He kissed the inside of her thighs. 'Don't forget the Sanatogen,' he winked.

They dressed. He opened the door, outside waited the faithful dog, soaked to the skin, he'd be glad when this screwing was over. Mellors held up the lantern, she looked into his strange eyes; fancy, two pounds thirty shillings, would he ever be able to break the habit.

'It's quarter to seven, you'll do it,' he said.

Yes, I'll do it, she thought, and why not, he's just done me.

'I'll come tomorrow,' she whimpered.

'Aye,' he said. 'Not so late, I want to get back to eight a second.'

Suddenly he grabbed her, whipped his hand up her dress and felt her fanny, the hairs on it were like bristles, as he let each one go they went Pinggg! Oh, they're going to do a knee-trembler thought the dog and started to howl.

'Please don't kick his arse,' she begged and was gone into the night. He returned to his cottage for a pleasant hour of sewing on fly buttons. There's an old country saying: 'There's nowt like it.'

The next day she didn't go to the woods because of a big surprise. She went out instead with Clifford. He could occasionally go out in the car. He had got a strong man as a chauffeur – he was so strong he could lift a bar bell 399 pounds in weight above his head and leave it there! So he could lift Clifford out of the car if need be – there were frequent 'needs be', you can't live in a car. He went to see Leslie Winter at Shipley Hall.

Winter was an elderly gentleman and had been since he

was seven. He was a wealthy coal owner, he owned three 100-cwt sacks. He'd had his heyday in King Edward's time, it was very nice of Edward to let Winter have his heyday in the King's time. King Edward had stayed at Winter's for the shooting, but each time the old man had hidden. Winter, his home was a handsome Georgian stucco villa. He prided himself on his style, which was in a field a mile away, but the place was beset by collieries: there was one in every room. Winter did not entertain much respect for Clifford because of photographs in illustrated papers, especially the *Exchange and Mart*! Towards Constance he was always gallant, but that was only *towards*: sideways and backwards he was different. He thought her an attractive, demure maiden, he was no judge of character. Dr Crippen had been the family doctor. Constance wondered what he would say if he found that Lord Chatterley's gamekeeper was having intercourse with her. Would it be, 'Stop that,' or 'Pull that thing out Mellors'? Winter gave her a rather lovely miniature of an eighteenth-century lady, rather against her will, in fact the eighteenth-century lady asked for it back.

But Constance was worried about her affair with the gamekeeper. At that moment he was in his cottage further reinforcing the buttons on his flies.

> If you go down in the woods today
> Beware of a big surprise
> For there inside the wood you'll find
> He who has reinforced flies.

She did not go to the woods that day in case of a big surprise. For days she didn't go. She refused to go and open her thighs to that man. He'd have to use a crowbar. To distract herself, she thought of all the things she could do: she could canvas for Hercules Drought, the Liberal MP, salmon fishing on the Tay, prospecting for oil in

Kent, have another mug of Sanatogen and a spoon of Keplers Malt; she resisted all these and did the Charleston instead to a record by the Wolverines.

Next day she went for a walk in the woods but in the opposite direction to people seeing her, like Norris Creep. She would only appear to be going in a direction, there was no sign it was an *opposite* direction. It would be a waste of public money to put up a sign saying 'OPPOSITE DIRECTION' but it would have been informative to Norris Creep. Suddenly, she heard a dog bark, Bow-wow: yes, that was a dog. Her heart beat, was it *his* dog, she stood on tiptoe, her ear cupped to listen for the traditional dog's kick up the arse, but no! it was the white bull-terrier from Marehay[37] Farm. Mrs Flint the farmer's wife ran out.

'Why, it's Lady Chatterley! Why.' Yes, it *was* Lady Chatterley! Why! She shouted at the dog. 'Down Brick Shithouse, down!'

'He used to know me,' said Constance shaking Mrs Flint's hand.

'Of course he knows you,' she said. 'He's just showing off. He understands every word you say,' she said.

'Oh,' said Constance. She turned to the dog and said, 'six hundred BC was the golden age of Greece, during which time there was Socrates, Xenophanes and Euclid.' She waited. 'He doesn't seem to understand,' she said.

'It's a long time since you've been 'ere,' said Mrs Flint. 'I do hope you're better.'

'Better?' said Constance. 'I haven't been ill.'

'Oh, that's why you look better,' said the farmer's wife, voted Idiot of the Year on a show of hands at Gonville and Caius College, Cambridge, the same vote one day they would give the Governor General of the BBC.—

'We've hardly seen you allll winter,' she said.

[37] Where does Lawrence get these strange un-British names, *vide* Wragby etc.?

'What a coincidence,' said Constance. 'We've hardly seen you allll winter.'

'Will you come in and look at the baby?' said Mrs Flint.

Constance went in and looked at the baby. 'Now what?' she said. She remembered she had sent the child some celluloid ducks for Christmas. The Flints ate them.

Mrs Flint picked up the baby. 'There! Who's come to see you? Who's this? Lady Chatterley – you know Lady Chatterley, don't you?'

How right Gonville and Caius College were.

'I was just going to have a rough cup of tea. Would you care for a cup? I don't suppose it's what you're used to.'

'No,' said Constance. 'I'm used to a blend of Lapsang Sou Chong and Lychee-Black.'

'Oh,' said Mrs Flint, who Gonville and Caius had also voted Ignoramus of the year.

She started re-laying the table, the best tablecloth, best cups and the best teapot. It still looked bloody awful. Constance had a cup of tea; it was jet black, she sipped it, ran to the window and spat it out.

'Don't you like it?' said the idiot of the year.

'Oh yes, it was lovely, it's just that I like spitting tea out of windows, it's a family custom, it's supposed to get rid of evil spirits.'

'Oh,' said Mrs Flint. 'We know how to get rid of evil spirits. We drink 'em. My husband makes them from sloes.' Constance squirted another mouthful of tea out of the window.

'It's not much of a tea,' said Mrs Flint.

'No, it isn't,' said Constance. 'I must go, my husband has no idea where I am.'

'Tell him you were in England,' said Mrs Flint.

'He'll be wondering all kinds of things,' said Constance. Strangely, at that moment, Clifford was wondering all kinds of things. He was thinking of fire engines and elephants: the first could put out a fire quickly, and the second, could, given the time, mind you, it would be pointless to give an elephant the time.

At last Constance rose and gradually came down again. 'Goodbye,' said Constance.

Mrs Flint insisted on opening the locked, bolted and barred door, so did Constance. After two hours Mrs Flint said, 'It's no good, it'll have to be the window.'

Mrs Flint accompanied Lady Chatterley down the lane, for this she brought her banjo. They came to a little gate, Mrs Flint insisted Lady Chatterley opened it. On the other side stood an empty milk bottle.

'Ah that's our milk bottle,' said Mrs Flint, 'the dairy man fills it and leaves it there for us.'

'When do you collect it?' said Constance.

'Oh, any time,' said Mrs Flint, 'May, September.'

'Doesn't the milk go off?' said Constance.

'No, it never goes off, it always stays where it is.'

The *Northern Echo* reported the gate incident.

LADY CHATTERLEY OPENS GATE
FOR HUMBLE FARMER'S WIFE.
'I can't believe she did it,'
says 52-year-old farmer's wife.

As Constance walked away she could hear the man calling up the last cows. Constance had never seen cows go up before or for that matter down, but she had seen them going along. Mrs Flint went running back across the pasture, in a sun-bonnet, because she was really a school-teacher.[38]

Constance thought of Mrs Flint's baby. Yes, Mrs Flint, though only a poor farmer's wife, had something Lady Chatterley hadn't got. Crabs. She was startled out of her muse, gave a little cry of fear, 'Aeroughh argggg elouw!!!'

---

[38] This D. H. Lawrence sentence baffles me. Does it mean if farmers' wives want to become school-teachers they have to wear sun-bonnets or vice-versa?

A man was there, it was the gamekeeper and, my God, he had a crowbar!

'How's this?' he said, holding it up. He moved forward and squeezed one of her boobs.

'Ouch,' she said.

'Do you really mean ouch?' he said with a leer.

'I must go,' she said. 'I must run.'

Before she could must run, he barred her way, it didn't take long to install them. 'Give me the slip eh?' he said.

'I'm sorry I'm not wearing one,' she said.

She felt his body near to her, was that him or his crowbar? Her old instinct was to fight for her freedom like Joan of Arc.[39]

'Come through here,' he said.

Suddenly a strange weight was on her limbs, he attached them to slow her down. He took her through a wall of dense, prickly fir-trees; they were young and not more than half grown. When fully grown to, say, thirty feet they were chopped down and used as telegraph poles, and were a very profitable industry, especially in Scotland where there were large plantations. The gamekeeper took her to a clearing in the wood.

> There was a man who was no good
> Took a maid into the wood
> Bye Bye Black Bird
> There he took off all her clothes
> Electric boots, her drawers, her hose
> Bye Bye Black Bird
> Then he took her where no one could find her
> With a rope he tied her hands behind her
> Then he laid her on her back
> Stuck his willy up her crack
> Black Bird Bye Bye.

[39] Burnt by the English, they were terrible cooks.

He threw his overcoat on the ground, then her. He made her lie properly, properly (?). Yet he broke the band of her underclothes.[40] He bared the front of his body, and she felt his naked flesh against her as he came into her, Woosh! For a moment he was still inside her, turgid there and quivering. Wow! Then he started to move, it was the Oxford Cambridge boat race all over again. In! Out! In! Out! In! Out! In the sudden helpless orgasm, there awoke in her new strange thrills rippling inside her. Rippling, rippling, rippling, oh Christ! Whoopee!!! She lay unconscious of the wild little cries she uttered at last. Yyeioow! Zowie! Wheee! She clung to him, he never quite slipped from her, actually he did but before he noticed it she whipped it back in. In! Out! In! Out! He was up to forty strokes a minute and passing under Mortlake Bridge. They were now both enveloped in a cloud of steam.

Lord Chatterley was at home having honey for tea. He said to Mrs Bolton, 'Constance is awfully late. I wonder what she's doing.'

She wasn't doing anything, the gamekeeper was. The shag was over, and she lay there crying, giving unconscious inarticulate cries, 'Yeeleedooo! Ninghtinggg! Peeiowieee!'

'For Christ's sake, shut up! We don't want him, his wheelchair an' his gun coming?'

Suddenly the weather was cold, very cold, his things were all shrivelled up, you could strike matches on them. He stood up and put his vest on. Lying there she looked up and saw his wedding tackle looming above. All was silent save the dog tied to a bush, who was grateful for the shag, knowing the longer they shagged, he wouldn't get his arse kicked.

'We came off together this time,' said the gamekeeper.

She did not answer. Doing a lot of it can make you blind and deaf.

[40] Please somebody explain! S.M.

She said, 'Do people often come off together?'

'Many of them never, only trains and buses.' She didn't know what he meant, neither did he.

'Have you come off like that with other women?'

'Come off like what?'

'Like that.'

'Like that?'

'Yes.'

'Yes what?'

'Like that.'

'That what?'

'Yes.'

She watched his face and the passion for him moved in her bowels, and she let one go. He put on his waistcoat and coat.

'No,' he said. 'It's Lent, I'm a Catholic.'

'Aren't you going to out your trousers on?' she said.

'I don't understand,' said the naked mistress.

'Well, in Lent, we're supposed to give up something, I'm giving up trousers.' The last rays of the sun touched the wood. 'I won't come with you,' he said. 'Better not, don't want to be bloody well shot.'

She watched her lover depart, a ray of sunshine hit his bum.

The next lines are all D. H. Lawrence; at the end I will ask a question.

Connie went home slowly, realizing the depth of the other thing in her. Another self was alive in her, burning molten and soft in her womb and bowels! . . . She adored him, till her knees were weak . . . In her womb and bowels she was flowing and alive . . . she realized the immense difference between having a child to oneself and having a child to a man whom one's bowels yearned towards.

Why is Lawrence so involved with bowels?

Simply, after two shags with the gamekeeper, she adored him. She was all bowels and sexual fantasy. Ah yes! O to be like a Bacchanal.[41] O to flee scantily clad through the woods[42] to call on Iacchos, the bright phallos (was it floodlit?) that had no independent personality behind it (what's happened to the gamekeeper?). Oh! let not man intrude, he was but a servant, the keeper of the bright phallos, her own. (She wanted one of her own.) These days she had but to enter a sex shop and buy a good Japanese vibrator.

The old passion flamed in her for a time, man dwindled to a contemptible object, something like John Major is today. The mere phallus-bearer, to be torn to pieces (possibly then a kebab?) She felt the force of Bacchae in her limbs and body (and presumably the bowels), the woman gleaming and rapid, beating down the male, perhaps using a hammer like Mellors. She would like to sink in the new bath of life, in the depth of her womb and her bowels.

'I had tea with Mrs Flint today,' she said to Clifford.

'You didn't drink it,' he said worriedly.

She shook her head. 'I saw the baby, it's adorable, with hair like red cobwebs.'

'How terrible,' he said.

'I saw you go across the park,' said Mrs Bolton.

'Of course you did,' said Constance.

Mrs Bolton was almost sure she had a lover. Where was that man? That man was in his cottage washing out his semen-stained underpants, occasionally using a cheese-grater.

'I've invited the Flints to tea,' she said.

Clifford grabbed his chest as though he had a heart seizure. 'Invited them?' he gasped. 'What for?'

'To see the baby.'

At this he slid from his wheelchair to the floor. 'The baby with hair like red cobwebs?' he said.

[41] Noisy, drunken revelry.
[42] In this country she'd get pneumonia.

'Yes.'

'Oh Christ.'

Mrs Bolton hoisted him back into his chair, her charge was a modest two pounds. The cheque should be made out to Boltons Haulage & Co.

'Don't you want to see the baby?' said Constance.

'All right, but I don't want to sit through tea with it.'

'Oh,' said Constance.

She didn't really see him, he was somebody else, she wasn't sure who to choose, finally she settled on Mr Stuart Wilson, a surgeon serving in the 7th Hussars during the Crimean War.

'You have tea with Mrs Flint in your room, my lady,' said Mrs Bolton. 'I'm sure Mr Wilson in the Crimea would prefer that.'

Constance didn't take her bath that evening, instead she took her gas stove. The sense of his flesh touching her was dear to her and in a sense holy, like the Sermon on the Mount, or even dismounted.

Clifford was very uneasy, he kept thinking he was Stuart Wilson, a surgeon in the Crimea. After dinner he said to her, 'You smell nice, was it the bath?'

'No, it was the gas stove.'

She thought she heard cannon fire emanating from him. 'It's the Crimea,' he explained.

After dinner, would she like to play a game, 'Or shall I read to you?' he said.

'I'll play hide and seek,' she said. 'You read.'

He read out the First World War Armistice of restrictions and limits imposed on Germany. 'Listen to this. They are not allowed any submarines. Destroyers are limited to eight in number with the limit of three-inch guns.'

As the cannonade in the Crimea grew louder, Clifford had to raise his voice so Mrs Bolton put bricks under the wheels of his chair.

'Cooeee!' said Constance who was hiding in the pantry. 'Guess where I am.'

'The library,' he said.

'No, but you're getting warm,' she called.

'You hear that, Mrs Bolton, bank the fire down a bit.'

'Cooeee!' When Constance called again she had moved further away. 'Where am I now?'

'The Crimea?' he said.

'No,' she giggled. 'You're getting colder.'

'Mrs Bolton,' he said. 'Stoke the fire up again.'

Aloud he read how Germany was only allowed two battleships of under 30,000 tons and no aircraft.

After that Constance shouted, 'Do you give up?'

He only nodded but loudly but she heard it above the noise of the Crimean cannons. She came out of hiding. 'I was in the wine cellar,' she said.

Clifford went on reading the terms of the Armistice aloud, 'German bicycle platoons mustn't have wheels.'

Inside her she could feel the humming of passion[43] like the sound of bells.

'You rang, my lady,' said Mrs Bolton.

Her answer was drowned out by Clifford's blaring voice. 'All German Admirals who partook in the War are to be taken out to sea and sunk by naval gun-fire.'

He went on reading in a louder voice, yet she had heard not a syllable. He looked at her for a moment. She fascinated him helplessly, as if some perfume about her intoxicated him,[44] what she was smelling of was gas. Clifford's voice grated on about the banning of Zeppelins, military balloons and carrier pigeons.

She was like a forest, humming with the sound of opening buds (it was bells, now its buds). She was in the same world as her man, beautiful with the phallic mystery. Yes,

[43] Time for another shag.
[44] She had had a gas stove rather than a bath.

he certainly had a beautiful phallic mystery, twelve inches of it.

Clifford's voice went on, clapping and gurgling with unusual sounds, 'Thulggg! Kragonk! Xacactx!!

Suddenly she realized he had stopped reading the terms of the Armistice and was improvising!

'Clifford, what are you doing?'

'I was just testing to see if you had been listening.'

'Of course I was,' she lied.

'Then what have I been saying?'

'You said Thulggg, Kagonk, Xaxacts.' It was an inspired guess.

'I'm sorry I doubted you,' said Clifford. He went on full of confidence. 'Germany will not be allowed anti-aircraft guns but they can throw stones.'

Mrs Bolton brought in two glasses of malted milk for Clifford to make him sleep, and Constance to fatten her again. Clifford drank his and crashed to the floor in a deep sleep, Constance drank hers and immediately to her horror she put on a stone. She shook Clifford awake to say goodnight, sleep well. She didn't kiss him goodnight. The cow, he'd spent two hours reading the Armistice terms of the First World War and no kiss! He'd teach her! Tomorrow he'd read her *T-Kreigshat-Mullers Treatment of Haemorrhoids among Kurdish Homosexuals* by Professor Richard Inghams! He gazed coldly and angrily at the door whence she had gone, the door took the full force of it.

And again the dread of night came on him, he had a dead willy he couldn't work. Coincidentally, like the gamekeeper, he had tried hitting it with a hammer with no result. He thought how cold Constance had become: otherwise why had she put extra blankets on her bed? Life was a terrible hollow somehow, actually it was a workman's hole outside the front door into which he kept crashing his motorized wheelchair. Energyless at times he felt he was dead, really dead. To verify this, every day he got them to lie him in a field with a shovel by his side. Nothing much happened except a Martian approached and left his card.

He couldn't sleep at night. But now he could ring for Mrs Bolton. She couldn't make him sleep either. She made him a coffee, sold him a packet of biscuits and sang him the Seventy-Ninth Psalm. 'Fear not the night for they that go must surely come back, and as wherefore so they shall. Verily it will be thus after.' They played piquet, she bet sixpence; Lord Chatterley £100,000, Wragby Hall and 120 acres of arable land. She never won, so she stayed on. As they played she thought of her Ted, long dead – quite long: he was nearly seven foot. She had a grudge against the masters who had killed him, like Lloyd George. Lloyd George did not kill Ted, he was nowhere near him. No, Ted was in the canteen. Suddenly there was an air raid, German planes started dropping exploding tea urns and one fell on Ted.

Playing cards with Mrs Bolton made Clifford forget himself. He kept asking her who he was. He was winning, he was up sixpence. With his sex life, he was happy to be up anything.

Constance was in bed fast asleep. While at his cottage, the gamekeeper was sitting close by the fire and thought he could smell burning. He was right, it was him. The brigade came and put him out. Continuing, scorched black, he thought of his wife, he hadn't seen her since 1915, yet she was not three miles away, not three but two. He *could* have seen her – all he'd to do was get on his roof with a telescope and focus on her windows. If he did it at eight o'clock of a Monday evening he'd see Bill Grongler the coal-man screwing her against the kitchen sink, before delivering a hundredweight of best nuts. I mean he could take a Thermos and sandwiches up on the roof and watch it all the way through. He hoped he'd never see her again as long as he lived; it would be very hard to afterwards. He remembered his days in India and his narrow escape from

death during a tribal attack. He was hiding in the NAAFI
under a table with a tea urn on it, when a cobra struck at
him but just missed him and bit the tea urn. That tea urn
had saved his life, he was so grateful he bought the tea urn,
and brought it back to England with him, where it now
took pride of place: Derbyshire. He recalled his old Indian
Army sergeant, but he was too far away to hear, and his
colonel who had died of pneumonia for his country.

Those days had gone, now he was in England a civilian
gamekeeper. His job was to raise pheasants so he raised
them up three feet. He had left being an officer and was
back among the common people where there was no
pretence. A penny more or less on the bacon was terrible,
especially for the Jews who bought it disguised as Catholics.
And the call for higher wages was a futile cry, there was
no solution short of death, but, there was no shortage of
death, only money.

Ah! But here in a Derbyshire forest he felt safe, no
Afghan tribesman could find him here, but they were
fiendishly cunning, so he kept his rifle at the high port as
he ran behind tree after tree. He was thinking, what did he
care about money? Nothing! Even though he needed a
fresh sock, so what! He could carry on with just one, not
only was he carrying on with one sock, he was also
carrying on with Lady Chatterley. He was ten years older
than she, but she was a stone heavier. In the silence of these
woods he was thinking of Lady Chatterley. He would
have given *all* he had to be with her. That would be: one
walnut veneer wardrobe, one kerosene oil stove, one second-
hand pine table, one fireside stool, one dog basket, one
iron Army-style bed, one tick mattress, three blankets, one
oil lamp, one zinc bath, one zinc bucket with broken
handle, one bedside mat (worn), three pairs of underpants,
three vests (need of repair), one sock, parrot cage empty
(parrot died), one meat-safe, one washing-board, one banjo,
two pairs ex-officers pyjamas, two pairs trousers (*sic*) one

pair in constant use, one face-flannel, one bar Sunlight
soap, one bottle Anzora hair-cream, one comb (teeth missing), one hair-brush, one sink pump, one frying-pan, one
ex-Army overcoat (button missing), one doormat, one
coal-scuttle, one packet Quaker Oats, one slice bacon, one
egg, one knife, fork and spoon, half a pound of prunes,
one tube Colgate toothpaste, yes, all that he would have
given. The trouble was getting a furniture-van to move it
at this time of night.

Like a maggot (*sic*) he was drawn towards Wragby Hall.
He saw a light in the house go on. He did not see Mrs
Bolton come to the window. She started, there was a man
out there, a black figure in the twilight; you rarely saw one
in Derbyshire unless it was a coal-miner who hadn't
washed!

Mellors was looking for an entrance to the house: if
only, if only the key-holes were bigger. He tried forcing
his head through one but it was useless. Ah! Up there was
her window, it was *open*, she was waiting for him! By the
house lay a long pole. That's it! He would pole-vault into
her room. Securing their love blanket to his hands he
started to run.

Mrs Bolton saw the man flash past, launch himself up,
up, up, he missed the window, but not the wall, against
which he crashed, fell back senseless, where fortunately the
ground broke his fall. The sun was getting up, so was the
gamekeeper, but nowhere as bright. As he got brighter,
Mrs Bolton saw it wasn't a black man but Mellors! So! *He*
was Lady Chatterley's lover. He, He. Why, she had been a
tiny bit in love with him herself but she had never shown
that bit to him, although he often asked to see it. When she
was studying, he had helped her a lot with anatomy, he
felt all her important parts. He'd been clever at school, he
learned French and things, 'La plume de ma tante est dans
le jardin' and things he could say. He'd been a nice lad and
helped her. He was clever at making things clear to you. 'If

you jump in front of a train it will kill you.' At the zoo he pointed at a lion. 'If you go in his cage he will kill you, I'll show you.' He threw his mother-in-law in and the lion ate her. 'See what I mean . . .?' At college he passed with honours. He became an overhead blacksmith[45] shoeing horses from overhead.

Well, well, so her ladyship had fallen for him, she must have seen his lovely white loins. Mind you, she wasn't the first: there was something about him. A huge prick.

He, as the day grew on, realized it's no good trying to get rid of your aloneness; he was all right until the parrot died, he had to admit he tasted delicious. You've got to stick to your aloneness. At times that gap may be filled, like when the dog comes in. With a sudden snap Boinggg! his bleeding desire for her broke, and he felt a bleeding sight better. There must be a coming together of both sides, like ladies' corsets. He turned slowly 360 degrees, which brought him back to where he started. No! She must come to *him*, it was no use trailing after her. But he'd have one more try. Taking the pole he ran, halfway up the pole snapped. No, she would have to come to him.

Mrs Bolton watched him limp away.

[45] I have no idea how this job is performed, Lawrence doesn't say.

ELEVEN

THE CHATTERLEYS were a family that all suffered lumbar problems. So Constance was in the lumbar room sorting it out. She unwrapped the old family cot. She had to unwrap it to look at it. A powerful intellect at work, she looked at it a long time. Three days. 'It's a thousand pities it won't be called for,' said Mrs Bolton. True, in all the years she'd been here, no one had ever called for the cradle.

'It might!' said Constance. 'I might have a child.'

'But', said Mrs Bolton, 'Sir Clifford . . .'

'Oh that,' said Constance. 'It's only muscular paralysis – it doesn't affect *him*,' she said, lying. 'They transfer the seed.'

Clifford had put the idea in her head. 'Of course, I may have a child yet. The potency may even come back . . .'

He had tried everything, pornographic photographs, dipping it into a glass of hot Guinness, he had a black woman come and massage it with mustard and rum. A French woman came and danced the Charleston naked for him. He had hung it out of the window with the sun on it. Finally, he hit it with a mallet, to no effect, but it left him with happy memories.

If Constance had a child it would not be his.

'Transfer the seed?' said Mrs Bolton. 'How do they get it?'

'I think it's done manually,' said Constance.

Mrs Bolton was flabbergasted, this is a condition when one's flabber is gasted.

'My word,' said Mrs Bolton. 'A child in Wragby, what a difference it would make. No one will get a wink of bloody sleep.'

Among the other monstrosities in the lumbar room was an elephant's-foot umbrella-stand. Constance thought how cruel to leave an elephant with only three and a half legs. Mrs Bolton thought it wonderful.

'Then you have it,' said Constance.

'Oh your ladyship,' said Mrs Bolton. 'I'll never be able to thank you.'

'Oh, what a pity,' said Constance. 'If I'd have known that I'd never have given it to you.'

Mr Bells drove her and her elephant's foot to her home, showing her friends. They all started to whisper about Lady Chatterley's baby (amazing the effect an elephant's foot can have on people).

'Wonders'll never cease,' said Mrs Weedon.

'Oh, wonders *do* cease,' said Mrs Bolton. 'Look at the Pyramids, they've ceased, and what about the Hanging Gardens of Babylon?'

'Have they ceased as well?' said Mrs Weedon.

Back at Wragby the vicar was having tea with Lord Chatterley. 'May we hope for an heir at Wragby?' he said.

'We may hope,' said Clifford, who at that moment had his willy in a battery-heated wooden splint trying to revive it.

One afternoon old Leslie Winter called, he was every inch a gentleman, his grand total was $77\frac{1}{4}$ inches. He owned a coal-mine and had bought a sack of it for Clifford. 'They're the very best nuts,' he said.

'Thank you,' said Clifford, who wished he had some of his own.

'What's this about there being an heir at Wragby?' said three inches of the $77\frac{1}{4}$ inches.

'There's hope,' said Clifford, throwing a best nut on the fire.

Old Winter came across the room to Clifford, it took him an hour. 'Congratulations,' he said and wrung Clifford's hand.

'You rang, sir,' said Mrs Bolton.

Old Mr Winter was very moved, together they moved him into the street.

'Constance,' said Clifford, as he played with Mr Winter's best nuts. 'There's a rumour you are going to bear a son and heir.'

'No,' she said. 'Is it a joke?'

'Well, I can't see a funny side. I hope it's a prophecy,' he said.

'Beware false prophets,' said Constance. 'Remember John the Baptist prophecy, John: X, 6, line 3: "They that cometh with the fish must surely goeth away, and they that bring not fish, will beat their breasts knees and teeth, and lo it will be Friday."'

Clifford stayed silent. Constance was arranging yellow tulips in a vase.

'Father wants me to go on holiday to Venice with them, won't you come too?'

'I won't travel abroad,' he said. 'Lewisham is as far as I go. How long will you be there?'

'Five foot seven,' she said.

'Five foot seven,' he repeated. He looked through his conversion table. 'Five foot seven, that's twenty-one days. I suppose I could stand three weeks.'

'My God,' thought Constance, 'on those legs how is he going to stand for three weeks!' She was thinking of the man with the blanket.

'I should like to see Venice again,' she said. 'But I loathe the Lido!'

Clifford was stunned, he wheeled his chair so close to her he could see up her nose. 'All these years I've known you and I never knew you loathed the Lido.'

'Are you sure you won't come nearer than Lewisham?' she said.

He gave a wan smile. 'No, just think of me at the Gare du Nord: at Calais quay!'

She promised him she would.

'Why not come,' she said, taking the tulips across the room to the window and throwing them out. 'It wouldn't be a difficult journey, we'd motor all the way.'

'I'd never be able to keep up in a wheelchair,' he said.

Very well. She reckoned that if she had a child he'd think she'd had a lover in Venice. For a hundred lire any gondolier would screw you and chuck in a couple of arias free, and a Give-it-to-me ice-cream. She went for a ride, Field driving her. She passed grim-looking shops selling soap, rhubarb, Anzora haircream and lavatory brushes. There was a chapel or two, a shop or two and cocktails for two. The country rolled away, south towards the Peak, east towards Mansfield and in the far distance the dome of Lewisham Hippodrome. Constance was travelling south, how it was hard to say, as the car was going north. They passed miners coming home from work, some of whom that might be poaching Clifford's rabbits and salmon. Mind you, she didn't like them poached, but grilled, yes, many miners were caught grilling rabbits and salmon. They drove through Shipley Deer Park on Mr Winter's land. He said miners were not as ornamental as deer, but far more profitable. He had an open season on miners to thin them out. Mr Winter told her he no longer went for walks in the park; only recently he had been butted by a miner during the rutting season. 'He crupled my blurzon,' he said showing her the bruise on his blurzon. It happened when he was wearing patent-leather shoes and purple silk socks; alas! they didn't save him. He had read an advert 'Wear Harrods' silk purple socks and avoid attacks by rutting miners'. He felt guilty about being rich, but nothing would change his lifestyle, only death.

This happened soon after Constance's visit. His heirs at once ordered Shipley Hall pulled down, perhaps that's what killed him, he was still living in it. He remembered Clifford in his will, he didn't leave him any money, but he remembered him. A Shipley Hall estate sprang up, no one, but no one, would have dreamed that Shipley Hall once stood there. Strangely enough, Mrs Bolton dreamed that Shipley Hall stood there. She dreamed it two nights running. At midnight Constance saw her in her nightdress racing round and round Wragby.

Constance could see the buildings spreading into the fields, and the new erectum rising at the collieries.[46] At the Pally, new girls in their silk stockings were dancing the depraved fox-trot with young louts.

'I dropped off for tea with Miss Bentley,' said Constance.

'Did she ask after me?' said Clifford.

'She *worships* you. St George of Cappadocia was nothing to you in her eyes.'

'She must have very bad eyesight.'

'She ranks you higher than Nurse Cavell.'

'Higher than Nurse Cavell? She's dead and buried six foot down. Of course I'm higher.'

'Miss Bentley is a darling. Why don't men marry women who adore them?'

'Women start admiring men too late, they should start about ten-thirty, ugly women should start earlier.'

'Clifford, do you realize you are the *Roman de la Rose* of Miss Bentley and lots like her!'

'Are they in lots?' he said. 'Can you bid for them?'

'You are cruel.'

'And who was the Roman of the Rose?'

'Oh, it's just a saying.'

'I know, I heard you saying it.'

[46] All original D. H. Lawrence stuff.

She went upstairs to change, but when she came down she still was the same person.

That evening he said to her. 'Look, if you go to Venice you won't have a lovely affair . . .' here he referred to a French dictionary '*au grand sérieux*, will you?'

'A love affair in Venice *au grand sérieux*. No, I'd never take a love affair in Venice more than' she referred to her French dictionary and read '*au très petit sérieux*'.

He knotted his brows then cast off.

Coming down next morning Constance found the keeper's dog Fred was in the hall with his arse against the wall so she knew Mellors was near.

'Why Fred?' she said.

'Why not?' said Mrs Bolton. 'What's in a name, a rose by any name would smell as sweet.'

'Was that Shakespeare?' said Constance.

'No, that was me, Shakespeare's dead,' said Mrs Bolton, jokingly.

Constance went to Clifford's bedroom, he was in bed, but oh! standing at attention at the foot of the bed was Mellors.

'Oh,' said Constance. 'I didn't know you were busy.'

What was she talking about? He wasn't busy, he was in bed doing bugger-all.

'Say good morning to Mellors, darling,' he said.

'Good morning to Mellors, darling,' she said.

She slipped out of the room again, it was oil on the floor. From her window she saw Mellors leave, he was Clifford's hireling. The fault, dear Brutus, is not in our stars, but ourselves, we are underlings. Was Mellors an underling, certainly he was under six foot, underpaid and now under her window. He looked up, she waved at him, he ignored her. Fuck him, thought Lady Chatterley. Three-thirty! It was time for her Isadora Duncan dance.

In the garden she talked to Mrs Bolton. 'Is it many years since you lost your husband?' she said.

'Twenty-seven,' said Mrs Bolton. 'We've looked every-where for him.'

'Did you try Lewisham? Lots of husbands get lost there.'

Reflectively Mrs Bolton said, 'He was a bitter man.'

'Oh! did you taste him then?'

Mrs Bolton burst into floods of tears.

'The flower beds. Try and cry on the flower beds, Mrs Bolton, there's a hosepipe ban,' said Constance.

TWELVE

AFTER HER Isadora Duncan dance she went to the chicken hut in the woods. He wasn't inside, he wasn't outside, the truth dawned on her, he wasn't there, and there was no blanket on the floor, she stifled a sob. So to his cottage. He was at his table eating. Seeing her, he arose, still eating.

'May I come in?' she teased.

'Grobilley-grid-gron,' he said, his mouth full.

'Please don't stop eating because of me,' she teased.

So he didn't stop eating because of her. On the table was a plate with potatoes, they looked like King Edwards which could be had for sixpence a pound. There were the remains of a six-ounce chop, that would be one shilling and threepence. He went on to speak, 'I think . . .'

'No, no, do go on eating,' she said.

The cottage loaf, that would be a penny.

'I had to go to Wlhwait,' he said between mouthfuls.

'Oh, don't stop eating because of me,' she teased.

He took up the chop bone, she could hear it cracking and crunching inside his mouth as the bone split, the grinding of his molars on the bits. Suddenly he coughed and three teeth flew out.

'It is lovely here,' she said, posing by the window.

He started eating again. As the bits of bone went down, she could hear them lacerating the inside of his throat.

When he finished screaming and kicking the dog he said, 'Can I stop now?'

She smiled. 'Can I take your plate away?'

'No,' he said, hiding it under his jacket. 'It's the only one I've got.'

Suddenly he thought he heard someone. 'Fred!' he said to his dog. 'Go out and hark! hark!' The dog trotted out to reconnoitre and hark! hark!

'Next month I'm going to Venice,' she said.

'Venice?' he said. 'Isn't that where the water is?'

'Yes,' she said, then in a low voice said, 'I've told Clifford I might have a child.'

Mellors dived under the table. 'D-d-did you mention me?' he said.

'No,' she said.

'Then how are you going to have a child?' he said.

'I might have a love affair in Venice,' she smiled.

'That'll be like German lager.'

She was puzzled. 'Like German lager?'

'Yes,' he said. 'Fucking near water,' he laughed.

'So far,' she said, 'I've taken no precautions against having a child.'

'Well,' he said, 'if you want to, I can always use a length of bicycle inner tube.'

There was a long pause of silence, a cold silence. They had to light the fire.

'Would you like to go upstairs now?' he said, lowering his trousers.

'No! No! Not here, not now,' she said heavily.

He pulled his braces up. She stood close to him.

'I've never really touched your body,' she sighed.

He looked at her. 'Now then?' he said, lowering his trousers again.

'No, no, not here. At the chicken hut. Romance was ablaze.'

She put on her hat. 'Goodbye,' she said.

'You'll be going in the woods,' he said.

'Only if I'm desperate,' she said and was gone.

He put his erection on the table and hit it with a mallet.

She walked home downcast, her knickers aflame. She got back to Wragby Hall, but was no good, she could neither sit nor stand, she would have to do something about it, she crouched, and went around the house like Quasimodo. She would *have* to go back! Like the Indian love song, the chicken hut was calling her. She slipped out the side door, it was that same patch of oil. In the distance she could hear chickens clucking, how her heart raced. There he was stooping over the chickens knocking off eggs for his breakfast.

'You see I've come,' she said.

'You don't want me to start eating again, do you?' he asked anxiously.

She didn't answer.

'Why', he said, 'are you hunched up like Quasimodo?'

'Oh, I'd forgotten,' she laughed, straightening up. 'I didn't want Clifford to think it was me leaving the house.'

'Oh,' said Mellors. 'You wanted him to think it was Quasimodo.'

She nodded.

He stood up, straightening his back. 'Arrrrrghhhhhhh,' he screamed, holding the base of his spine.

'What is it?' she said anxiously.

'It's Arrrrrghhhhhh,' he said. He swallowed a bottle of aspirins. 'It'll soon go,' he said.

Lady Chatterley was genuinely worried, about his back. Could he screw like that?

'Shall us go i' the 'ut,' he said.

My God, thought Constance, he's gone into the vernacular. They went inside, he brushed away the chicken shit and laid the blanket down.

''Ave you left your underthings off?' he asked her.

'Yes,' she said. 'They're at the laundry.'

'Aye, well then I'll take my things off too.' He took off his shoes, one sock and trousers. 'Lie down,' he said.

He stood over her in his shirt, she looked up and saw what looked like a plucked chicken. He then sprang on her, he started fiercely fondling her breasts, it was more like an osteopathic massage.

'For God's sake, go easy,' she said. 'You'll have them off!'

'Ee but tha'rt wa' nice.'

Yet more of that terrible vernacular! She put her arms around him under his shirt, seeking for his skin. Alas! in the way was his Army vest. As he banged away, his contracting and uncontracting buttocks seemed ridiculous to her, he was gradually, she realized, thrusting her up the blanket to where all the chicken shit was. He noticed it and pulled her back again. Hadn't this all happened before? Indeed it had. (See p. 405.) The whole thing seemed ridiculous to her. Her impulse was to heave her loins and throw him off into the chicken shit.

Soon it was all over, he lay back, she could see steam rising from his massed genitalia. He gave her a slight laugh.

'Someone asked me,' he said, 'did I smoke after sex, and I said I'd never looked.'

How could he joke about something so sacred, but who was she to argue with a man who had the biggest prick in Derbyshire.

'Th'art good cunt, though, aren't ter.'

'What is cunt?' she said.

'Cunt! It's thee down theer,' he said, rubbing up her pubic hairs.

'So,' she said. 'Cunt! It's like fuck.'

'Nay, nay. Fuck's only what you do. Animals fuck. But cunt's a lot more than that.'

'It's time I was going,' she said.

THIRTEEN

SUNDAY. Clifford wanted to go into the wood. Poor Clifford who had to be lifted from his bed into his wheelchair, into the bath, out of the bath, on to the toilet, off the toilet, into his wheelchair. That wasn't too bad, but they kept dropping him. Connie still suffered having to lift his inert legs into place, it got her in the small of her back. His motor wheelchair came puffing into view.

'Sir Clifford on his throbbing steed.' This was what upper classes thought of as a witty line.

'Snorting at least,' laughed Constance. This was also meant to be an upper-class witty line. There was more to come. Clifford stopped and looked at the house.

'Wragby doesn't blink an eyelid,' (Eh?) he said, then came an even more profound utterance. 'But then why should it? I ride upon the achievements of the mind of man, and that beats a horse!'

And from her this. 'I suppose it does. And the souls in Plato riding up to heaven in a two-horse chariot would go in a Ford car now!'

Came his witty retort. 'Or a Rolls-Royce: Plato was an aristocrat!'

'Yes, yes,' she said laughing. 'And instead of horses only an engine and gas.'

They both hooted with laughter. If only they had a few bread rolls to throw.

Constance didn't really want to go to the woods, once you'd seen one tree you'd seen them all. If she'd been a dog she'd have felt differently. So she walked beside his chair in a certain obstinacy of spirit.

'Why are you walking beside me in a certain obstinacy of spirit?' he said.

'I was worried – they say some of the miners are striking,' she said.

'Oh,' he said in a puzzled voice. 'Well, I've seen all my miners and none of them looked striking to me.'

'I feel guilty about their poverty and our riches,' she said.

'That is fate,' he said. 'Why is the star Jupiter bigger than the star Neptune?'

'Because', she said. 'Neptune is smaller.'

What a *silly* man he was, in frustration she stamped her foot on the ground, killing an ant (*Lasius niger*).

'But you own the mine, you're responsible *for their lives*.' She stamped her foot, making the dead ant flatter.

'Yes, I do own it,' he said. 'But ownership of property has become a religious question since Jesus and St Francis.'

'Jesus never owned any property.'

'No, he was a bloody awful business man.' He stopped his motor wheelchair. 'Look,' he said and pointed to a tree.

To humour him she looked. 'And there's another,' he said. 'The woods are full of them! They are on my property,' he added angrily. 'Just wait till I find the owner.'

Constance waited for him to find the owner. He was saying there would always be rich and poor. There was something devastatingly true in what he said. But it was a truth that killed.

He had spoken the truth to Herbert Lunge and it killed him. Clifford stopped the chair. 'Beautiful,' he said. 'What is better than an *English* spring?'

Constance thought it sounded as though the spring

bloomed by an act of Parliament. An English spring? Why
not an Irish one or a Jewish? At least with a Jewish one
you'd get a discount.

Seeing her pale and silent, he started up his motor chair,
obscuring her in choking clouds of carbon-monoxide. Clifford drove his chair to the tip of a five-hundred-foot drop.
Constance followed slowly behind, the temptation was
great, one good push, and his policy would mature. The
oak-buds were opening, so were the pubs, in the distance
she could hear the rush of alcoholic boots.

'Shall I venture as far as the spring?' said Clifford.

'This *is* the spring,' she said. 'This is May, can't you
remember?'

'I meant the well spring, water, can't you remember?'
he said. 'Surely you can tell the difference between the
month of May and water coming out of the ground.'

He pulled down his racing goggles, he revved up the
engine using the noise to obscure a tremendous postern
blast that nearly lifted him out of the chair. It reached
Constance.

'My God,' she said. 'There's a dead body somewhere
around here!'

He drove off at fifty miles an hour leaving her behind
with it.

Constance heard a low whistle behind her. She turned, it
was the man with the biggest one in Derbyshire. "As 'ee
got a gun?' he said, white with fear.

'No,' she said.

'Oh, good,' he said, taking off his false beard and
moustache. 'I'll see you tonight, I've had the blanket
cleaned.'

'Yes,' she said.

With both hands Mellors pushed her breasts up from
underneath, up to underneath her chin, with a cry of
'Wheeee', and let them fall down and bounce to a halt.
'Wheeee' he said and did it again.

'Look,' said Constance. 'That's enough of that, I'm not a bloody fairground.'

'Peep peep pee,' came the sound of Clifford tooting on his horn.

'He's calling me,' she said.

'What's wrong with his voice?' said Mellors.

'That's *not* his voice,' snapped Constance. 'Can't you tell the difference between Lord Chatterley's voice and a motor-car horn?'

'No,' he said. 'I can't, but I make up for it. I can tell the difference between the month of May and water coming out of a hole in the ground.'

She shrugged her shoulders and of all things her nose.

She found Clifford slowly climbing to the spring, he was halfway up the slope and by sheer coincidence halfway down as well. When she reached him he had arrived at the spring – he pointed at it with an obstetrical finger.

'See? How *could* you mistake that for May?' he said.

He noticed a paper bag she was carrying. 'It's bread rolls,' she said. 'I brought them in case you wanted to throw some. Remember how at college dinners you used to throw them?'

He smiled in recollection. 'Yes, it was jolly fun.'

'Remember you blinded Anthony Deeds,' she said.

He laughed, 'By jove yes.'

She took an enamel mug from a nail on the tree,[47] took water from the spring and sipped it. 'Mmmmm,' she said, then handed the mug to Clifford, he drank it.

'Did you wish?' she said.

'Yes,' he said. 'I wished I hadn't drunk it, it was bloody awful.'

'Oh,' she said. 'Would you like to throw a bread roll at me?'

Right at their feet a mole appeared. 'Unpleasant little beast, we ought to kill him,' said Clifford cocking his gun.

[47] There was a 100–1 chance of finding this.

'No, no, it's bad luck,' she said.
'Only for him,' he said.
'No, no,' she said.
'There's an old Derbyshire poem:

> If a mole you do kill
> Thou shall get very ill.'

'Rubbish,' he said. Taking aim he fired both barrels, the mole disintegrated. Immediately he got bronchitis. 'Quick! a bread roll,' he said, grasping one and eating it. Something was wrong, thought Constance.

Lord Chatterley was baffled. How could a dead mole give you bronchitis?

They started on the return journey. They came to the dark bottom of the hollow. It was the darkest bottom he'd seen since Josephine Baker's at the Folies in Paris. 'A black ars'ole' as his company sergeant had described it.

'Now, old girl,' said Clifford putting his motor chair into gear, he revved the engine again, using the noise to mask another giant postern blast, when it reached Lady Chatterley she fainted. She recovered to see the motor chair struggling to get up the hill. She stayed her distance in case he let another one go.

He was crouched forward, revving the engine, he engaged the gears. '*Now*, old girl,' he shouted.

'Now what?' shouted Constance.

'I wasn't talking to you,' he shouted. 'It was the chair.'

The engine was racing flat out, gradually he was obscured in clouds of dense smoke.

'Are you all right in there?' called Constance. The smoke cleared. There sat Lord Chatterley tense, white-faced and with a nose-bleed.

'Shall I push you?' she said.

'No, that won't stop it, you need a key down my neck,' he said in a rage.

Constance rummaged through her handbag, no keys. 'I've only got this ladies silver-backed hairbrush, would that do?'

Clifford snatched it, rapidly he brushed his hair. 'It's no good, it's not stopping it,' he said. 'Fancy having a bleeding nose, like mine,' he said.

'Oh,' said Constance, 'I've seen a lot bleeding worse.'

In the silence that followed, a pigeon started to coo roo-hoo, coo roo-hoo, its delicate sound floating on the evening air. Lord Chatterley gave it both barrels, with a thud it hit the ground.

'It's dead,' sobbed Constance.

'Ah, the fall must have killed him.'

He tried to start the engine up again, a series of splutters and bangs then stopped. 'Did you hear that? It gave a series of splutters and bangs then stopped.'

Should she give him a bread roll?

'If only I could get out and look at the damned thing,' he said.

'Well, *I'm* out here looking at the damned thing,' said Constance, 'and it doesn't seem to make much difference. Look, would you like me to describe it to you?'

Oh, why did he marry her, there was a time when he could have married Mademoiselle Marie la Taché of 15 Rue de Lyon, Paris.

The gunshot had alerted Mellors and his smooth white loins. He came running. 'I heard a shot, I thought ah! poachers.'

'There are no ah! poachers,' said Lord Chatterley. 'It was me.'

He pointed to the dead bird. Mellors stared, picked up the bird showing the tag on its leg. 'That's my prize racing pigeon,' he blurted.

'I'm sorry, Mellors,' said Lord Chatterley. 'I'll see it won't happen again.'

'Of course it can't happen again,' said Mellors. 'It's dead.'

'I'm very, very sorry. I'll see you are compensated. Meantime, don't waste it, have it for dinner.'

'That's very kind of you, your lordship,' said Mellors, respectfully saluting, knowing in a few hours he would be fucking her ladyship.

'Do you know anything about motors?' asked Clifford sharply.

'Do *I* know anything about motors!' repeated Mellors.

'Look man! *I'm* asking *you*!', said Clifford, using his handkerchief to wipe the last of the blood from his nose.

'I'm afraid I don't, sir, if it had been racing pigeons . . .'

Lord Chatterley wasn't driving a racing pigeon.

'Can you get underneath and have a look?'

Mellors, on his back, pulled himself under the chair.

'Can you see anything?' said Clifford impatiently.

'Not from under here,' he said. 'The chair's in the way.'

Lord Chatterley fumed, why did he employ idiots?

'The engine seems all right,' came Mellors' muffled voice.

'I don't suppose you can do anything,' said Clifford.

'Yes, I could come out,' said Mellors.

Lord Chatterley, like a rabbi, beat his breast in frustration.

'Is it indigestion dear?' said Lady Chatterley.

He regained his composure. 'Mellors?'

'Yes, sir,' came the voice from under the chair.

'I'm going to advance the ignition. I want you to see what happens.'

Advancing the ignition he pressed the starter, there was a loud bang and the engine throbbed into life.

'Has anything happened?' he shouted to Mellors.

'Yes!' shouted Mellors. 'My shirt's caught fire.'

The smouldering Mellors came out from under the chair, his face blackened with oil.

'Oh, I am sorry,' said Clifford sympathetically.

'You're sorry,' said Mellors.

The engine stopped. 'Can you give me a push?' said Clifford.

Mellors gripped the back of the chair and as he did the engine burst into life. Alas! it was in reverse and ran backwards over Mellors.

'What are you doing down there?' said the enraged lord.

'I'm getting up, sir,' said Mellors.

'You're no good to me down there, man,' said the heartless lord.

He revved up the engine. Suddenly, without warning, the chair shot sideways, jettisoning the crippled lord into a ditch full of water.

'Someone will pay for this,' he raged.

'No, darling, it's all free,' said Constance as she and Mellors pulled the bedraggled lord out.

Together he and Constance tried to get his lordship into the chair.

'Will you stop your bloody dog barking at me,' fumed the lord.

He took a swipe at the dog which turned and bit one of his dead legs.

Mellors shouted, 'Heel, heel.'

'Don't say *that*!' said the lord. 'He's just bitten my heel.'

Mellors gave the dog a kick up the arse.

'It's no good, the chair will have to be pushed,' said Clifford with an affectation of *sang-froid*.

Constance winced at his *sang-froid*, doing it in French didn't fool her, she knew it meant composure of mind; imperturbability; freedom from agitation! [Fr. *sang* blood; *froid* cold].

Mellors went to push the chair, but only propelled himself backwards. Mellors was ten stone, Lord Chatterley was eighteen: an eight-stone advantage. Even adding Mellors' two-stone dog, Lord Chatterley still had the advantage, even adding his six-pound dead pigeon wasn't enough, with this six-stone eight-pound disadvantage.

'Do you mind pushing me home, Mellors my man?' said Clifford in a superior disdainful voice.

Never mind, thought Mellors, 'my man', tonight he would be fucking Lady Chatterley, that should even things up. He took a firm grip on the chair and pushed. He took a firm grip on the chair and pushed. He grip on the chair firm and on. He on chair the grip push on he. Push he on grip took firm chair.

'What's stopping you, Mellors?' said Lord Chatterley.

'It's you and the chair, sir,' Mellors said.

'Is it too heavy?' said Constance.

'No, your ladyship, it's not too heavy. I'm too light,' he said.

Mellors would have one more try. Rolling up his sleeves, he spat on is hands but missed, it landed on the back of Sir Clifford's neck.

'Something's landed on my neck,' said Sir Clifford.

'It's only some spit, darling,' said Constance soothingly.

'What's spit doing on my neck?' he said.

'It's, not doing anything,' she said.

'How did it get there?' he said.

'By travelling,' she said.

Why, oh why, did he marry her? He could have married anybody, he did and it turned out to be her.

At last Mellors heaved the back of the chair off the ground, with one foot he tried to loosen the wheels, but the six-stone eight-pound disadvantage activated and the chair sank back. Clifford was clutching the sides.

'I'll take a run at it, my lady,' said Mellors.

He walked back a good fifty yards, turned and started a run gathering speed as he neared the chair. Alas, he missed, shot past it and collided with a tree.

'Thank you, Mellors,' said Sir Clifford. 'But that hasn't been much help.'

Mellors explained his next plan. 'If my lady pushed this wheel while I pull the other.' He heaved while she tugged, the chair reeled.

'For God's sake,' cried Sir Clifford in terror.

Too late, the brake came off, the chair started to run backwards down the hill.

'Some one stop it,' shouted the disappearing lord.

Mellors and Constance set off in pursuit.

'The brakes, your lordship,' shouted Mellors.

He could see the lord struggling with them.

'Do as Mellors says, darling,' shouted Constance after him.

To make matters worse, the engine started up again. Mellors drew abreast of the chair and managed to put two stones under the wheels bringing it to a halt. Clouds of engine enveloped the hapless lord.

'Are you all right in there?' cooed Constance. 'We'll come in and see you when it's cleared.'

Mellors sat on a grassy bank gasping for breath.

'Are you all right?' said Constance.

'Aye, that pneumonia took a lot out of me,' he said.

'Oh, did you ever get any of it back?' she said.

He shook his head, but not normally, no it was manually operated. He grabbed each ear in a hand, then agitated his head from left to right.

Constance looked at him puzzled. 'Are you a Mason?' she said.

He nodded, this he did by grasping the hair on the back of his head, gripping his nose with his other hand and levering it back and forth. Both of these were secret masonic recognition signals to fellow masons. He told Constance he reached the level of the Red Cross degree and Babalonis Pass.

'Did you hear that, darling, Mellors is a Mason, he said he joined because it leads to big business city deals and banking.'

'Well, before that happens, can he push this bloody wheelchair home,' said Sir Clifford.

Mellors agreed to push the chair. 'Though', he said, 'it

will delay my entry into the world of big city deals and banking.'

He rose from the grassy bank.

'Can you carry this for me, your ladyship?' he said and handed her the dead pigeon.

'Are you ready, Sir Clifford,' said Mellors.

'Am I ready??!!' exploded Clifford.

'I don't know, sir,' said Mellors. 'Are you?'

'Look!' said Clifford. 'I'm a Mason too, if you don't start pushing, I'll write to your Lodge and have your Babalonish Pass annulled!'

Mellors took the stones from under the wheels. Taking hold of the back he gave the chair a push to the limit of his strength.

'Brother Mason, what are you doing back there!' said Sir Clifford.

An exhausted voice said,[48] 'I've just given the chair a push to the limit of my strength.'

'Is that why you're lying down?' said Sir Clifford.

The supine figure on the grass verge didn't answer.

'Is he dead?' said Sir Clifford.

'No,' said Constance tenderly. 'He's recovering from pneumonia.'

'Does he have to do it here?' he said angrily. 'Can't he do it at home?'

Mellors arose, 'I'm all right now, sir, just getting my breath back,' he said.

'Oh, it's back is it?' said the hardhearted[49] Sir Clifford. 'Off we go then.'

Again, like some race-memory, he took hold of the back of the chair. At an angle of forty-five degrees he strained to move the chair, he strained again and suffered a

---

[48] It would eventually give him a coronary.
[49] Ibid.

prolapse which he pushed back in by hand, but there was no 'Off we go then'.

'Why aren't we off we go then?' said an end of his tether Sir Clifford. In a moment of desperate anguish he said to Constance, 'Darling, do you think I will ever see my home again?'

'Don't worry, darling,' said Constance assuringly. 'We'll make it.'

'Yes, but will *he*?' said Clifford.

'Look, sir,' said Mellors. 'We'll make it if her ladyship helps push as well.'

Sir Clifford clenched his fists. 'My wife push as well!! Do you know what you're saying?'

'Yes,' said Mellors. 'I made it up as I went along.'

'But using my wife, a lady, as a *common labourer*! What would people say?'

'I'm sorry, sir,' said Mellors. 'I don't know what people would say.'

'Are you sure?' said Sir Clifford.

'Positive.'

'Well, somebody must know what people would say,' said Sir Clifford.

'Look, darling,' said Constance. 'I'm going to help Mellors, so please hold this.' She handed him the dead pigeon.

'Look, darling,' said Sir Clifford. 'I don't want you to push. I'm perfectly willing to stay here while you go and get help.'

'You can't stay here all night,' she said uncertainly.

'Yes, as long as you send some food out,' he said.

'What do you want?'

'Well, I'd like to start with Brown Windsor soup, then a fish course, grilled salmon, main course? chicken fricassée.'

'No, no, darling,' she protested. 'By the time it got here it would be cold.'

He mused. 'Yes, you're right, there's nothing worse than cold chicken fricassée.'

Sir Clifford wanted to murder Mellors.

'Have you ever eaten cold chicken fricassée?' queried Sir Clifford.

'Er no, sir, I haven't,' said Mellors.

'Well I *have*,' said the triumphant lord. 'And believe it *is* worse than pneumonia.'

'Begging your pardon, sir,' said Mellors respectfully. 'But have you ever had pneumonia?'

'No.'

'Well I have and it *is* worse than cold chicken fricassée. I mean pneumonia lasts two weeks, chicken fricassée wouldn't last that long.'

Constance interrupted, 'I gave my dog a cold chicken fricassée once and he finished it in five minutes.'

'Whose bloody side are you on?' roared Sir Clifford. 'Pneumonia or chicken fricassée?'

Shaking with fury he released his hold on the dead pigeon, it fell to the ground. In a flash Mellors' dog Fred had the bird tight in his jaws.

'Come here,' ordered Mellors. 'Give me that,' he ordered. 'Let go,' he ordered. 'Put that down,' he ordered. 'Stop that,' he ordered, to no avail. The sun was setting. Time was short. 'Good dog,' he said trying to pull the bird free, but Fred was not a good dog, he held the bird like a vice.

'I've got an idea,' said Mellors. He took ten paces back, ran and kicked the dog up the arse, the pigeon shot out the other end. 'Good dog,' said Mellors to the convulsed canine.

'Look,' said anxious Sir Clifford. 'It's getting dark.'

'I know,' said Mellors. 'It happens every night around here.'

Together Constance and Mellors continued to push the chair. He suffered a brief prolapse.

'Are you all right?' said Constance.

'Just a prolapse, my lady,' he said, pushing it back in.

As they pushed he glimpsed her milk white wrist and

the flame of strength went down his back and up his smooth white loins, agitating his wedding tackle.[50] In a brief pause she kissed his hand, the very one he had used on his prolapse.

'Why have we stopped?' asked the irritated Sir Clifford.

'It's Mellors, dear, he's had a prolapse.' She wanted to add, 'And he's squeezing my tits.'

'Oh,' said Sir Clifford. 'Here Mellors, this will make you feel better, have a pull at this,' and passed him his brandy flask.

Mellors pulled the flask. 'I'm pulling it, Sir Clifford, but nothing's happening.'

Sir Clifford took the flask, unscrewed the top. 'This is how you pull,' he said, then drank the flask dry and put it back in his pocket.

'There,' he said. 'I've made myself feel better for you.'

'Thank you, sir, I'll know next time,' said Mellors.

How cruel Clifford was, thought Constance. For the first time she hated him as if he ought to be obliterated from the earth. She would start by trying to obliterate him from Wragby, but it wouldn't be easy to obliterate a person, but with him she had a start, his legs were already obliterated.

Three prolapses later they were at the top of the hill and on to the flat.

'Look, I'm shagged out,' whispered Mellors to her ladyship. 'I can't fuck tonight.'

It was a shattering blow to her ladyship, who had worked all the positions out for that night including one against the gas stove.

Clifford was saying that Sir Malcolm had written to ask would Constance drive him in his small car to Venice. Constance laughed out loud. 'Drive a car to *Venice*,' she said. 'It'll sink!'

---

[50] Soldier jargon for sexual organ.

On the levée the gamekeeper could push the chair alone.

'I wouldn't like travelling by open car,' continued Constance. 'There's all that dust.'

'Well, you could take a duster,' said Sir Clifford chuckling.

'I'll see what Helen wants,' said Constance.

'Oh,' said Sir Clifford. 'She'll want to drive her own car and take you with her to inhale the dust,' chuckled Sir Clifford.

Mellors was struggling again.

'Let me help,' she said. 'God, you are heavy, Clifford.'

'Here this will make me lighter,' he said and handed her the dead pigeon.

She went to the back of the chair and pushed.

'Look,' said Sir Clifford. 'Why not let me wait and go and fetch Field? He's strong enough for the job. He can lift a gas stove above his head.'

Constance ran to Wragby and found Field in the kitchen.

'Are you strong enough to push Sir Clifford's wheelchair?' she said.

'Yes,' he said.

'Good,' she said. 'Then lift that gas stove over your head.'

Field took hold of the stove, he strained and strained to lift it, in the end collapsed in a heap sobbing, 'I can't do it, it's that Rita Lurch. I'm not the man I used to be.'

'Who were you?' said Constance with interest.

'I used to be the Reverend Norman Wooley, a vicar in Lewisham, then I met Rita Lurch.'

Gasping, Constance reported back to Sir Clifford. 'He can't lift gas stoves any more.'

'Oh dearie me,' said Sir Clifford grimly. 'I'll have to fire him.'

'Oh why, oh why?' pleaded Constance.

'Because,' said Sir Clifford, 'I won't have people working for me who can't lift gas stoves over their heads.'

'Mellors can't lift a gas stove over his head,' pleaded Constance.

'No, he slipped through the net,' said Sir Clifford. 'It's getting dark, we'd better call the police.'

'Will they make it brighter?' said Mellors.

Sir Clifford wanted to murder Mellors.

'Darling, it isn't far to go now,' said Constance. 'See.' With a tape she measured the distance to the front door. 'It's only twenty feet.'

'Sorry I panicked,' said Sir Clifford.

It was the longest twenty feet ever, actually it had been a mile, the tape measure was inaccurate.

'Thank you so much, Mellors,' said Sir Clifford when they reached the house. 'I must get a different sort of motor,' he said.

'Like one that goes,' said Mellors.

'Why don't you go to the kitchen and have a meal?' said Sir Clifford.

'I'll tell you why, sir, the food's bloody awful in there. There's a man in there who keeps lifting the gas stove over his head, and you can't cook on it any more.'

Sir Clifford looked thoughtful, it was misleading because he wasn't thinking or anything.

'Here, Mellors,' he said. 'Here's your dinner,' and handed him the dead pigeon.

'Thank you, sir. I'll give it to my mother,' said Mellors.

'Will she cook it for you?' said Constance.

'No,' said Mellors uncomfortably. 'She'll eat it raw.'

'Oh,' said Constance. Why is that?'

Mellors shuffled his feet and got the joker. 'Well, I don't want this to get out my lady, but I think she's turning into a werewolf.'

Constance and Clifford looked horrified. 'Is she taking anything for it?' they said.

'Yes,' he said. 'Raw pigeons.'

The Chatterleys couldn't believe it, not only could he

not lift a gas stove over his head but his mother was a werewolf.

'Has she been to a doctor?' they said.

'Oh yes, as soon as the signs started she saw Dr Jacobs.'

'What happened?'

'She tried to eat him,' said Mellors. 'He said she was anti-Semitic but she's much better now. She had a boiled egg this morning.' So there was hope for her.

'Before you go, Mellors,' said Sir Clifford. 'Have a drink on me.' He handed him a packet of tea.

Mellors saluted the mean bastard and left. Lady Chatterley was furious: there went her dick for the night.

Next day after an exhausting hour of Isadora Duncan she came down to lunch. She couldn't contain her feelings as all the containers were full.

'Why were you so inconsiderate to Mellors yesterday?' she said to Clifford.

'I give up,' he said. '*Why* was I so inconsiderate to Mellors?'

'Pushing you gave him twelve prolapses,' she raged.

'But they all went back in, didn't they?' he asked.

'Not without his help,' she said, beside herself with rage.

One of her spoke, 'That poor man Mellors had been ill with cold chicken fricassée – I mean pneumonia. If I were the working class I'd let you whistle for your service!'

'I don't mind whistling for service, listen.' Therewith he whistled a chorus of 'Roses Are Blooming in Piccardy'.

'There,' he said. 'That should bring even the deafest servant running!'

Constance boiled. This man had the emotional depth of a blocked drain or an Out of Order phone box.

'Poor Mellors,' she said with a stifled sob. 'If *he'd* been sitting in that chair with paralysed legs, and behaved as you behaved, what would you have done to *him*?'

'I'd have had him put down, why? His werewolf mother could have him for dinner.'

'As if he weren't as much a man as you are.'

'He *isn't* as much a man as me: he's only ten stone and I'm eighteen!'

'He's ten stone because you pay him starvation wages.'

'I pay him two pounds a week, a man can starve quite comfortably on that. He can always eat one of his carrier pigeons.'

'Have you no feelings, Clifford?' she said.

'You know I only have them from the waist upwards. Why, do you want to feel me?' he laughed.

She shook her head in disbelief. 'If I were Mellors I'd tell you to keep your two pounds a week.'

'Oh, that would be most welcome,' he said.

'You make me sick!' she said.

'Oh, would you like a bucket?' he asked.

'I'm utterly ashamed of you.'

She jumped to her feet, which were over in the corner.

'My father is twenty times the human being you are,' she said.

'He must be huge,' said Clifford.

She sat in stunned silence.

Clifford rang the bell for Mrs Bolton.

'Mrs Bolton,' he smiled. 'Will you take Lady Chatterley outside and put her under the cold tap.'

Mrs Bolton took Constance down to the kitchen. Standing there, his face red, his eyes standing out like the stoppers on a harmonium was Fields, swaying, with a gas stove over his head.

'I've done it, I've done it,' he gasped. 'Despite Rita Lurch.'

'Put that gas stove down at once, there's a dinner in it!'

Mrs Bolton took Constance to the tap. It was leaking.

'Is that dripping?' she said.

'No, it's water,' said Mrs Bolton.

Mrs Bolton plunged Lady Chatterley's head under the tap.

'Why is he doing this to me?' she sighed.

'*He's* not doing it me lady, I am.'

'Then why are you doing it?' queried her ladyship.

'Because he's not,' Mrs Bolton explained, a stickler for detail. 'You see with his legs, he'd never make it to the sink.'

'This is mental cruelty,' said my lady. 'I'll take him to court, I'll charge him.'

'What with, mam?'

'Drowning. I'd accuse him of drowning me. Would you be a witness?'

Mrs Bolton. 'I can't, mam.'

'Why not?'

'You're not drowned yet.'

Behind them a life and death drama was in process as Fields, his legs collapsing, tried to lower the gas stove. Halfway down he lost his grip and the whole stove crashed to the floor and shattered in all directions.

'Oh, my God,' shrieked Mrs Bolton as a piece landed on her foot. 'Tonight's dinner is in there,' she said, delving among the pieces. Like a miracle the dinner was intact.

Constance went to her room furious. She took the stairs two at a time, then three, finally six; nearly splintered in two, it inflamed and krupled her blurzon, she applied hot towels, she put on Pond's vanishing cream, and for half an hour it vanished. When it came back she marked it with a cross so Mellors would know where it was. She made her plans for the evening, he'd sweep the chicken shit away and put the blanket down. She didn't want to hate Clifford or his legs. She didn't want him to know anything about her, least of all being fucked by the gamekeeper. This squabble about how he treated the servants was an old one. Mellors had quite an old one. She found Clifford stupidly insentient, tough and indiarubbery (Eh?). Where other people were concerned. Some of the concerned people were Tom Loon, Dick Squats, Len Lighthower, Lord

Mountbatten and Eric Grins: those unconcerned were Mrs Gladys Scrote and The Reverend Notts of Rhodesia.

That night for dinner she wore her magnificent black velvet dress, she went down the stairs with grace, poise and dignity. It was sad when she tripped over the cat.

'Have you hurt yourself, dear?' said Clifford.

Through clenched teeth, lying face down on the carpet she said, 'No, I haven't hurt myself, darling.'

'Good,' said Clifford. 'Only masochists hurt themselves, I'm so glad you're not one.'

'Would you mind,' she said standing up, 'if I killed the cat.'

It took half an hour but he talked her out of it.

Mrs Bolton served the dinner.

'It's chicken fricassée,' she said lifting off the cover. 'I'm sorry to say it's cold as the gas stove is broken.'

Clifford stiffened in his chair and in horrified tones repeated, '*Cold* chicken fricassée? Why, why that's worse than pneumonia!'

Calming, Clifford called in Rogers their wine waiter. 'Ah, Rogers, have you got a Macon?'

'No, sir,' he said. 'Why should I? It's not raining.'

'What are you talking about?' said Clifford.

Constance explained it was a missing understanding over the dual sounding of nomenclature.

'Rubbish,' was all he said.

Why, oh why, did she marry him, she could have married anybody, she did, and it turned out to be him.

'Have you read Proust?' he said.

'I've tried but he bores me.'

'Any particular part?'

'The cover. I never got any further than that.'

'But he's really extraordinary.'

'Well, he bores me to death.'

'Then you ought to read him,' said Clifford with a grim smile.

Constance put on a pretend yawn, as obvious as a knee elephant charging. It was just a coincidence that at that moment in Africa at the Londalozi Reserve Lord Charles Portal was being charged by a bull elephant, but of course there was a time difference between the United Kingdom and Africa – in our wintertime Africa was two hours ahead. Constance was yawning at eight-twenty p.m. so Sir Charles was being charged at twenty-twenty African time. Constance didn't yawn again till she got to her bedroom at nine-thirty-two p.m., by then in Africa it was eleven thirty-two and Sir Charles Portal was dead, flattened by the elephant. He was so flat they would bury him in a large envelope.

Clifford continued his defence of Proust. 'I like his subtlety and his well-bred anarchy.'

With a bitter smile and her lips screwed up like a chicken bum, she said, 'I hope you're both very happy together.'

'All right,' he retorted, chewing painfully on the last of the cold chicken fricassée.[50] During this he realized that whereas cold chicken fricassée *wasn't* worse than pneumonia, it was more nourishing.

'Who do *you* admire as a man?'

What she would say would be a coincidence in a million.

'I admire', she said, 'Lord Charles Portal.'

'Is he an author?' puzzled Clifford.

'No, he expresses himself in a different way,' she said delicately.

'How?' pressed Clifford.

'He shoots elephants.' In England it was twenty-thirty-two, in Africa it was twenty-two-thirty-two, and Lord Charles Portal was being laid out in the mortuary. Under

---

[50] Scientist eventually discovered what cold chicken fricassée was.

Balfour he was Minister for Foreign Affairs – in fact he himself was having one with a Hindu girl.

'I don't see the point of shooting elephants,' said Clifford. 'Proust never shot one.'

'Of course not,' she stressed. 'Where are you going to find an elephant to shoot in Paris?'

'Does Lord whats-his-name *have* to shoot elephants?' queried Clifford.

Mrs Bolton brought in the dessert, vanilla ice.

'I'm afraid it's cold as well,' she joked.

Colder still was Sir Charles Portal on his slab in the blacked-out Victoria district mortuary. The elephant that had flattened him was drinking peacefully from the banks of the Limpopo River.

Constance continued the question of elephant shooting.

'They shoot them to keep the numbers down.'

'Are elephants numbered?' Clifford asked.

'Yes,' she said. 'When I first met Sir Charles he'd just shot elephant number nine.'

Clifford looked at her disbelievingly.

'Sometimes he hunted with elephant dogs,' she said.

'Dogs? Did they kill elephants?' he said with great suspicion.

'Yes,' she said.

'Wow,' he said.

'They wait,' she explained.

'Wait?' He was totally baffled.

'Yes, wait,' she explained. 'Elephants have to die sometime.'

For the record, though neither party knew, the elephant that had flattened Lord Charles was number 329, so he had avenged 328 of his fellow Pachyderm.

'What do they do with dead elephants?' said Clifford, even more baffled.

Constance thought, while spooning in vanilla ice cream.

'The natives eat them,' she said finally.

'It must take a long time to eat one,' he said.

She informed him that in an erudite article in the Royal Geological Society magazine it states. 'It takes a tribe four weeks to eat an elephant, they actually sleep by their dinner.' She gave a huge yawn. Clifford looking in could see her vocal cords, the uvula, her tonsils and great harp strings of saliva.

She went up to her bedroom, she minced up, one step at a time, she didn't want to stretch it. She thought of Mellors again and his smooth white loins. What was her beloved doing?

He had just finished washing his socks and was now cutting his toenails, he was using secateurs, great shards of toenail flew in the air like showers of arrows, some burying themselves up to a quarter of an inch in the floor, three hit the dog, pliers had to be used to extract them. That's what her beloved was doing.

Meantime she, naked in front of a mirror and using a bolster as a partner, tangoed to a record of 'Blau Himmel', by the Berlin Novelty Trio. How her body blossomed with regular fucking and Horlicks, no longer had she a grey sapless body with flat thighs, but her fanny still looked like a crow's nest. It was an unfortunate moment for Lord Chatterley to be wheeled in by Mrs Bolton.

'My God, Constance!' he said in a stunned voice. 'What are you doing with that bolster?'

'The tango,' she said.

In a choked voice he said, 'Well, will you stop doing it while I'm talking to you.'

She turned off the gramophone, for her it was a real turn off. Hastily she slipped on a back silk kimono but not before Clifford saw what he thought was a crow's nest.

'I don't understand you,' said Clifford in a baffled voice. 'One minute you're talking about dead elephants, next I find you dancing naked with a bolster.'

'Darling,' she said, lying back on the bed, another flash

of the crow's nest. 'Darling, what I'm doing are Doctor Fritz Steam-Schitz's music and remedial exercises for lower-back problems.'

'You haven't got any back problems,' Clifford said.

'I know,' she replied. 'But it's silly to wait till the last moment.'

Mrs Bolton wheeled a stultified Lord Chatterley from the room. What was a crow's nest doing in his wife's bedroom?

FOURTEEN

WITH HIM GONE she quickly changed into a tennis dress, tennis shoes, a Helen Wills Moody headband, a tennis racket and a bag of tennis balls. She slipped out the side of the house, she was soon up again. If she met anybody she'd say she was Helen Wills Moody on her way to victory at Wimbledon. The only danger was that someone should go into her bedroom during the night and ask her to play tennis.

When she got to his cottage he was hiding in the cupboard.

'Is everything all right?' he said, fear in his voice.

'Everything's fine,' she said.

'He didn't follow you?'

'No.'

As she walked there were scrunching noises under her shoes.

'It's all right, he said. 'It's only toenails.'

'You been playing tennis?' he said.

'No,' she smiled.

'I see,' he said.

It was a free country. If people wanted to dress up as tennis players who weren't going to play, that was their business. It's what made Great Britain great. His great aunt Doris Mellors used to dress as Queen Victoria to have a bath. Yes, Britain was a great country and his great aunt was still inside.

Constance was talking to him.

'Are you sure you didn't hurt yourself this morning pushing that chair?'

'Am I sure I didn't?' he said. 'Sure I did!'

He explained the prolapses, now prolapses take some explaining, it took him half an hour. Constance was a good audience, she only stopped him once to explain the word 'Jaxie'.

She asked him, 'When you had that pneumonia, what did it do to you?'

'It knocked me sideways,' he said.

'Did it take you long to straighten up?'

'Yes, they used block and tackle,' he explained.

'You ought not to make violent physical efforts,' she said.

'Yes,' he said. 'If I fuck I must only do it in two-minute bursts.'

She smiled and patted him. 'Don't worry, we'll keep a stop-watch by the bed.'

She plodded on in an angry silence.

'Did you hate Clifford?' she said at last.

'I did, I do and will.'

'Who's will?' she said. 'And why do you hate him?'

Mellors unravelled the grammar for her.

'I don't like Lord Chatterley,' he said. 'He's not my sort.'

'What sort is he?'

'He's that youngish gentleman with no balls.'

She didn't understand.

'What balls?'

'Balls! A man's balls!'

She pondered this.

'But is it just a question of that . . . balls?'

'When a man hasn't got that spunky wild bit in him, you say he's got no balls.'

She pondered this, then said, 'But Clifford *has* got balls. I've seen them, they're huge, like Granny Smiths.'

Mellors had no idea that Granny Smith had big balls, that was her husband's problem so he did not pursue it.

'I'll take off my shoes, they're wet,' she said.

'I'd better sweep up the toenail cuttings first,' he said, sweeping them into a pile that reached nearly a foot high.

She was warm near the fire; she took off her coat, he hung it on the door.

The countdown to the shag had started.

'Shall you have cocoa or tea or coffee to drink?' he said.

She paused and put her arm over the back of the chair.

'Have you got any Moët & Chandon Brut '21?'

'No,' he said, 'but I've got cocoa or tea or coffee.'

'I don't think I want anything,' she said looking at the empty table. 'But you eat.'

'Please don't start that again. I'll just feed the dog,' he said putting food in a bowl. It was the dead pigeon.

He sat on a chair to take off his leggings and boots. She caught a glimpse of his ankle, her heart raced. The dog was trying to work out how to eat a meal with feathers on.

'Do you like dogs?' she said.

'No,' he said.

'Then why do you keep one?'

'To kick his arse.'

He had taken off his leggings and was taking off his huge boots.

Suddenly, after crossing and uncrossing her legs to ease the tension, she said, 'Why do the working class wear boots and aristocrats wear shoes?'

'It's to keep their feet dry,' he said.

He didn't understand the question, she left it at that.

Above his head on the wall was a photograph of a young couple, it was Mellors and his wife.

'Is that you?' she asked.

'Which one?' he said.

'The man, silly,' she answered.

'Yes, that's me,' he said feeling ashamed.

'Do you like it?'

'No.'

'Then why do you keep it?'

'It covers a damp stain on the wall.'

'Why don't you burn it?' she said.

He took the photograph down.

'Good heavens,' exclaimed Constance. 'There's a damp patch on your wall up there.'

'Yes,' he replied. 'That's the one I was telling you about.'

He handed her the photograph, it showed a young fresh-faced man and a young plump woman, their expressions were the same as those on the *Titanic* as it went down.

'Have you been keeping this for sentimental reasons?' Constance said sympathetically.

'No,' he said. 'I've been keeping it to cover the damp stain on the wall.'

'Oh dear,' said Constance. 'It makes me feel guilty.'

Mellors didn't answer, he just wondered how anyone could feel guilty about a damp stain on a wall. But then women were strange. She handed him the photograph to burn. He took it out of the frame.

'Do you know how much this photograph cost in 1920?' he asked.

'No,' said Constance.

'What a pity,' he said. 'Neither do I.'

He tore the photo in half then quarters then in eighths then sixteenths then thirty-secondths then with sweat pouring, sixty-fourths, then with veins standing out on his

forehead he tore them into one hundred and twenty-
eighths.

'For God's sake, that's enough,' gasped Constance. 'Save
something for the fuck.'

He threw the pieces into the fire, it flared up. He peered
into the flames, he liked a good peer. One of the good
peers he liked was Lord Sainsbury, founder of
Sainsbury's.

'Did you love your wife?' she asked him.

'I find that hard to say,' he said.

'No, it isn't,' she snapped. 'I've just said it and it's quite
easy.'

He spat into the fire and put it out.

'Did you love Sir Clifford?'

'Did I love Sir Clifford?' she repeated slowly. After a
pause, about an hour, she said, 'I really don't know what
to say.'

He came galloping to her rescue. 'Say, the quick brown
fox jumped over the lazy dogs.'

Constance pulled back, she raised her eyebrows, about
an inch and a quarter he estimated.

'Why do I have to say that?'

He looked oafish, then a bit more, till eventually he was
a complete oaf.

'That sentence reminds me of my mother, she was a
typist and she said that sentence used every letter of the
alphabet.'

'Well,' she said sympathetically. 'There is a sentence that
reminds me of my grandfather. "That was six months for
indecent exposure".'

He relit the fire.

'I think I'll have that cup of tea now,' she smiled.

He rose to make it, somehow his dangling braces had
caught in the chair which rose with him.

'How do you like your tea?' he said.

'I like it very much,' she smiled . . .

While he made the tea she liked very much, she asked him about his affairs.

'The first one was a schoolmaster's daughter, but she wouldn't let me do it, so I bought a forty-five Colt revolver and I forced her. Then I met a Jewish girl, before she'd do it, she liked foreplay, so I'd do twenty minutes' begging, then a cheque for five pounds. I had to give her up as I became penniless. Then there was Sally. She didn't like it, when I was doing it she just ground her teeth, after three months she was toothless. Then came Berth Coutts. She wanted me to fuck her, so I fucked her like a good un. Too late! I discovered she was a nymphomaniac, she never stopped, night and day. I forgot what it was like to wear clothes, she never stopped for food, in between the fucks I tried to make a cheese sandwich – so little time – I had to eat it while we were doing it,' he said.

Fred the dog was coughing up feathers.

'So,' said Constance crossing her legs, 'when you did get a woman who wanted it, you got too much of a good thing.'

'Aye,' he said reflectively. 'In the sanatorium they made me sleep with my willy packed in ice to reduce the temperature, and the doctor said my foreskin was gone for ever.' He wiped a tear from his eye.

'How terrible for you,' she said, and then hopefully, 'is it all right now?'

He smiled, straightened his shoulder, patted his flies and said, 'Aye, it's back to normal.'

Back to normal? she thought. How could he call that prick twelve inches long *normal*!

There was a long silence, then he said, 'Seems to me that most women are Lesbians.'

'When you find out a woman is a Lesbian, what do you do?' she enquired.

'I get away as fast as I can, a 137 bus or 74A tram does it.'

'Do you think Lesbians are worse than homosexual men?'

'Yes, because I suffered more from them! I went to a doctor, I asked him what was wrong with me, he said "I'm afraid you're suffering from Lesbians".'

He looked pale and his brows were sombre, even his nose, teeth and ears were sombre, there were even traces of sombre on his trousers, it was one of the greatest concentrations of sombre in Derbyshire.

'Were you sorry when I came along?' asked Constance.

'I was sorry and I was glad.'

'Make up your bloody mind,' snapped Constance.

He made up his bloody mind. 'Yes, I was glad. But I must forget the rest, when I can't forget the rest, I want to hide under the table and die.'

What in God's name was he talking about?

'Why,' said Constance in that upper class voice he hated, 'Why do you want to die under a table?'

'Well,' he said as he rolled a cigarette. 'It's cheaper to die under a table than have a funeral.'

Shouldn't this man be Chancellor of the Exchequer, she thought, but Lady Chatterley was never a very good judge of Chancellors of the Exchequer.

He took out a brass lighter, he flicked it, a huge flame shot out and incinerated the whole cigarette in a flash of flame igniting the hairs in his nose.

'Quick,' she said. 'Run it under the cold tap.'

He thought it wonderful to have this medical help at such short notice, but the carbonized hairs in his nose gave vent to a fit of sneezing but such sneezes that lifted him a foot off the ground for nearly ten minutes. He appeared to bound round the room like a kangaroo. In the end Constance had to jump on his back to hold him down. It wasn't a good time in their love affair. Gradually the sneezing stopped.

'Oh dearie me, oh dearie me,' he said dabbing his watering eyes. 'That was terrible.'

'Oh, I quite enjoyed it,' she said as she dismounted from him. 'I haven't had a piggy back since I was young.'

Should he strangle her? He looked at his nose in the mirror, it was slightly burnt.

> Oh what a thing is a nose
> It grows and it grows and it grows
> It grows from your head
> While you're lying in bed
> At the opposite end to your toes.[51]

He turned, showing his nose to Constance. 'Does it look terrible?' he said.

'Yes, terrible,' she said. 'And even worse now it's burnt.'

Should he strangle her? He made some more of the tea she liked very much. He poked the fire, another poke nearer her. The dog Fred, exhausted by coughing up feathers, lay on his bed surrounded by them.

'We are a couple of battered warriors,' she laughed.

Warriors? He had no idea what she was talking about, whatever she meant it went over his head and hit the damp patch on the wall above him. Then he went outside awhile with the dog. She heard him kick its arse then come back in. He took the empty wooden frame of the photograph, broke it up and threw it on the fire. How much would that photo have cost in 1920?

She slipped over to him by the fire, sitting at his feet she looked up and could see right up his nose. She saw the devastation. She shuddered.

'Cold?' he said.

'No, horrified,' she replied.

[51] Permission of Desmond Milligan.

He held her close in the running warmth of the fire. He could feel his one-eyed trouser snake activating. Suddenly without warning she flung her arms around his neck clinging to him.

Through the embrace came his muffled voice, 'For God's sake you're suffocating me!'

'I just wanted to hold you,' she said.

'I want you to forget all those women in your past.'

'I'll try, I'll start by forgetting Bertha Coutts,' he said, then for some reason he said, 'There's black days ahead.'

He went on, 'Aye there're black days coming for all of us.'

'Is this a weather forecast?' she queried.

She looked at him. He was pale, his brows were sullen, yes his ears, nose and teeth were sullen too. There were traces of sullen on his trousers, it was the most intense concentration of sullen in Derbyshire.

It was getting late, so to activate him she said, 'You know I can't go home till morning. Clifford thinks I'm out playing floodlit tennis.'

They don't make husbands as stupid as that any more, thought Mellors. He put his arms around her and started an intense search of her body, down below he felt what appeared to be a crow's nest. He felt her breast, it was soft and warm, he estimated about seventy-two degrees Fahrenheit. They went quickly to bed for it was growing very chilly, already his were all shrunk up. They fell asleep doing it. They awoke at first light. Sunshine touched the curtain.

'Oh, do let's draw the curtain,' she twittered. 'The birds are singing. *Do* let the sun in.'

He slipped out of bed, his back to her. She saw his back was fine, the small buttocks beautiful bar a few pimples, the back of the neck was fine too, supporting a boil with a plaster.

'You are beautiful,' she said. Long overdue for glances, she held out her arms to him.

He was ashamed to turn to her, because of his aroused manhood, which stood out like a fifteen-inch gun on a battleship. He caught his shirt off the floor and draped it over his willy, it now looked like a washing line.

'No,' said Constance. 'Let me see it.'

He dropped the shirt and revealed this steaming 'pork sword'.[52]

She nearly fainted with joy. 'Oh! Oh!' was all she could say, then, 'Bring it here.' By the size of it, it was almost already there. 'How strange!' she said slowly. 'So big and so dark!'

There was something wrong with her sense of colour, this thing wasn't dark, it was bright pink with purple veins, like a circular map of England's inland waterways.

The man looked in silence down at the tense phallos. 'Ay!' he said at last, 'Ay ma lad! tha're theer right enough. Yi, tha mun rear thy head. Theer on thy own, eh? an ta'es no count o'nob'dy! Tha ma'es nowt o'me, John Thomas. Art boss? of me? Eh well, tha're more cocky than me an' tha says less. John Thomas! Dost want her? Dost want my Lady Jane. Tha's dipped me in again, tha hast. Ay, an' tha comes up smilin' – Ax'er then! Ax Lady Jane! Ay, th' cheek on thee! Cunt, that's what tha're after. Tell Lady Jane tha wants cunt. John Thomas an' th'cunt o'Lady Jane!'[53]

Not in the history of man has a man spent so much time talking to his own prick.

'Oh, don't tease him,' said Constance crawling on her knees on the bed towards him.[54]

Suddenly in a sergeant-major's voice he barked out 'Lie down! You hear me? Lie down!'

[52] Sailor jargon for penis.
[53] Original D. H. Lawrence.
[54] *Ibid.*

Did he mean his prick or Constance? She took it as her. Soon his spotty bum became a blur of speed thrusting him in and out of her ladyship, great droplets of steam and sweat fell from his balls, then it was all over. He withdrew from her with a sound of sink pump clearing a drain. She looked down, to look at the mystery of the phallos, oh no! It had gone, the giant throbbing had gone, in its place was a little bit of gristle hanging down.

'He's gone,' she sobbed.

'Na' bither 'ell be back,' assured her lover.

She took it in her hand, it looked for all the world like a three-day-old featherless sparrow. 'And now he's tiny . . .' she said. 'Isn't he somehow lovely! so on his own, so strange! (Eh?) . . . so innocent, you must never insult him (it used to be an it, but now it's him). He's mine too, he's not only yours, he's mine!'[55] (a fifty per cent controlling interest). She gave 'him' a squeeze to activate it.

He laughed.

'Blest be the tie that binds our hearts in kindred love,'[56] he said. Computed that means 'thars a good fuck lass!' She stroked his pubic hair, a shower of scurf fell out. 'That's John Thomas's hair not mine,' he said.[57]

Oh the sparkling Wildean wit of the man. 'John Thomas! John Thomas. A rose by any name would smell as sweet,' she crooned with the prick pressed against her cheek. Actually, it didn't smell of roses, rather it reeked of vaginal lubricant. Suddenly the prick surged and filled up like a party balloon, bigger and bigger it swelled, would it explode? In fear Lady Chatterley sprang back.

'Hur Hur,' laughed the oaf. 'There! take him then! He's thine!'

[55] *Ibid.*
[56] *Ibid.*
[57] *Ibid.*

He's thine! Wonderful Biblical parlance. Silently she lay on her back, opened her legs, revealing the crow's nest. 'Oh' was all she said when the great thing entered her and worked away like a piston on a steam train. Oh, why hadn't she brought the Vaseline!

He heard the seven o'clock hooters of the colliery. With his face between her breasts he pressed her soft breasts up over his ears, he just grabbed one in each hand and stuck them in his ears.

Bloody nerve using her tits as earplugs. 'What's the time?' she said.

But with her tits in his ears he couldn't hear. Pulling them out she asked again. He didn't answer, he ran his hands through the hairs on her crow's nest. As he did they twanged like plucked harp strings.

After a while he reached for his shirt and put it on. How lovely he looked in his shirt with just the tip of his prick showing, oh how she loved him, he put one sock on. With his shirt, the tip of his prick and one sock on, he was her Adonis! Adonis went on to put his trousers and boots on. She heard him clumping around downstairs, it was like music to her ears clump clump clumpity clump! Ah Delius!

She had not heard the hooters. She lay perfectly still, her soul washed transparent without the aid of washing powders. She came mincingly downstairs, her crow's nest a bit sore, she'd have to camomile it when she got home.

He was washed and fresh, but last night had taken its toll, he kept having to sit down with dizzy spells. There was a fire.

'Will you eat anything?' he said.

'No. Only lend me a comb.'

He gave her one, she ate it.

'I would like the rest of the world to disappear,' she said in a state of ecstasy.

'Oh,' he said. 'Thats would mean goodbye to the Lewisham Hippodrome *and* Billy Bennett.'

She didn't care, all she wanted was, she clasped her hands together and breathed the word 'us'. But alas! one of 'us' had to go and feed the chickens. In a phallic trance she went back home in her Helen Wills Moody tennis clothes, she carried a net of tennis balls, but having seen Mellors these meant nothing to her. Back at Wragby she climbed the stairs.

FIFTEEN

THERE WAS A letter on the breakfast tray.
Strange – usually it was porridge. She opened
the envelope in case there was any breakfast in
it. It was a letter from Hilda saying her father
would call for her on the seventeenth of June,
she hoped she would hear him.

Most days Clifford was at the pits, sometimes it was a
colliery, but most people called it the pits. Conversation
with him was difficult, all he did was to listen to Christopher Stone on the wireless.

She told him at length she was leaving on the seventeenth.

'I'm telling you at length I'm leaving on the seventeenth,'
she said.

'The seventeenth,' he repeated. 'When at length will you
be back?'

'At length the twentieth of July.'

'At length the twentieth of July,' he repeated.

What was wrong with him, why was he repeating
everything.'

'Donkeys tootletums stuffed with straw,' she said.

'Donkeys tootletums stuffed with straw,' he repeated.
He wasn't well.

As he talked he was tearing out paper dolls from the
Derbyshire Times. She was quivering, watching her real
opportunity for leaving him altogether, although as was he
looked far from altogether.

She talked to Mellors about going abroad. He had never heard of Venice, but then nobody in Venice had heard of him. When she came back, she was going to leave Clifford.

'What will you say to him?' asked Mellors.

'Goodbye,' she said. 'Then we can go away anywhere, Paris, Rome, where would you like?'

'Well I'd like ter go to London. I've got an aunt living in Bargery Road, Catford. I'd like to see her.'

He took a photo from the mantelpiece 'showing twenty people of all ages'.

'Oh, are they all still alive?' she asked.

'Oh yes,' he said. 'You have to be alive to have your photo taken.'

'Oh,' said Constance a mite disappointed. 'Why shouldn't we go to South Africa or Australia?'

'Because my auntie isn't there,' he said.

'Oh, wherever,' she said. 'We'll be happy! We won't be poor. I have six hundred pounds a year!'

Ah, how easy it was to fuck your way to riches, he thought. Perhaps if he fucked her more the amount would go up!

'You've been to the Colonies, haven't you?' she said attentively.

'Yes,' he smiled. 'I bin to India, South Africa, and Egypt.' In each of these places he'd caught a packet.

'You were an officer and gentleman,' she said gushingly.

Yes he was, but even then he caught the crabs.

'Aye, I liked my Colonel but then he was killed.'

'And weren't you happy as an officer and a gentleman when your Colonel was dead?'

'It wouldn't look very good being happy as an officer and a gentleman, with your Colonel lying dead. Mind you, men who were officers and gentlemen who owed him money were happy.'

'Did you mind very much when he died?' said Constance.

'Yes, I was minding much of the Regimental silver.'

That's not what Constance meant, however she asked him, 'How did the Colonel die?'

He shrugged his shoulders, surely he didn't die by shrugging his shoulders?

'They say,' said Mellors, 'it was a sniper's bullet, others say it was a NAAFI tea urn.'

He told her his Colonel hated the middle class. 'My Colonel hated the middle class,' he said.

There was a sudden burst of thunder, when it had gone Mellors crawled out from under the table. Yes, the middle class were a 'generation of ladylike prigs with half a ball each'. He sat there in the hut, he was listening to the storm, he had one ear set backwards, it looked strange with the other ear facing the other way.

'The world will come to an end with everybody going insane before they do,' went on this newly found prophet. 'They'll make their *auto da fé*. You know what *auto da fé* means?'

Constance had a guess. 'It means automobile for sale?'

Without warning she pulled open his clothing, she laid her cheek on his belly and could clearly hear his lunch of lamb chops, boiled potatoes and peas going down, she gathered his balls in her hand and rolled them together.

'Ow,' he yelled. 'That bloody hurt.' It killed a delicate moment of romance.

'I'll kiss them better,' she said putting ruby lips to a wrinkled sack of skin with varicose veins and odd hairs.

There fell a complete silence. Constance started to thread forget-me-nots through his pubic hair. With a grand gesture with her left hand, the other holding his willy she said, 'Your love-hair is like a brush of bright red-gold mistletoe. It's the loveliest of all!' she said, feeling the ghost of Keats inspiring her.

He looked down, embarrassed, he had never been praised for his pubic hairs before. This woman had an eye for beauty.

She went and opened the door. She looked at the heavy rain, suddenly the rain god called her. He must have called her a nutcase for she ripped off her clothes and ran screaming into the deluge, she left behind her lover with forget-me-nots in his pubics. Alone in the rain she did her eurythmic Isadora Duncan dancing.

He was not slow to react: here was a chance of a fuck in the rain. Ignoring the threat of pneumonia, he threw off his clothes and ran after the woodland nymph. He caught her by the forget-me-nots. She gave a shriek, lying her on her back among twigs, slugs, snails, bird-droppings, he screwed her. The rain streamed on them till they smoked. He gathered her 'lovely' heavy posterior, one in each hand and pressed them towards him in a frenzy. The dog Fred stood by barking encouragement. Then wham bang! it was all over. He stood up with this huge thing steaming, gradually starting to droop, the rain running off it like a leaky gutter.

In the splendid surroundings of Buckingham Palace dining-room, enjoying their dinner, did King George V and Queen Mary dream that two of their devoted public, one an aristocratic lady was lying naked, being screwed by her gamekeeper with a twelve-inch-long phallos, during which they slid a hundred yards from their starting point. They now stood up covered in slugs, worms and frog spawn. As they ran back, his willy shrank till it looked like one of those strap hangers on the tube train. He was totally baffled, did all landed gentry females run naked and fuck in the rain? He realized why most gamekeepers never left their job.

The lovers sat drying themselves by a post-coital fire. He stroked her.

'Tha's got the nicest arse of anybody! And if that shits

and pisses I'm glad (*He's* glad!). I don't want a woman as couldna shit nor piss.'

He had been an officer and a gentleman. He admired her body, the roundness of her buttocks! And in between, folded in the secret warmth, the secret entrances. He really was a dirty devil. With quiet[58] fingers he threaded forget-me-nots in 'the fine brown fleece of the mound of Venus'.[59] These were early days of flower-arranging. He stuck a pink campion among the hair.

'There,' he said, 'that's Moses in the bulrushes.'

That Moses should be reduced to this.

'You don't mind me going to Venice?' she said cautiously.

His face went inscrutable, there was no sign of a scrute. There was silence. He put another log on the fire. The fire flared up showing his silent strong face. A large spark shot from the fire landing on his bare foot.

'Ow Christ!' he screamed, leaping around the room holding the burnt foot.

'Quick, run it under the tap, she said.

A man does not look his best from the back with one foot up in the sink with it all hanging down. Calm was restored. He made some cheese sandwiches. There came a terrible crack of thunder. With a cry of 'Duck' he threw himself face down on the floor. It was a throwback from shellfire during the war.

Constance didn't understand. 'Duck?' There was no sign of duck as he lay prone and a spark flew out on to his arse. He shot up with a scream.

'Quick, run it under the cold tap,' she urged.

Will she ever forget the sight of that man trying to get his arse under the cold tap. She had seen acrobats putting their heads between their legs and looking at their own

---

[58] Quiet fingers? What's Lawrence mean?

[59] D. H. Lawrence.

backside. Now here was her lover doing it. When it was
over he was reduced to sitting on one buttock, so he was at
an angle of forty-five degrees.

She put her arms around his neck and he toppled over.

'When I come back from Venice, will you take me
away?'

'Where?'

'Well, your aunt in Bargery Road, Catford.'

'We couldn't stay there long.'

'Why not?'

'She's a sado-masochist: every hour you have to tie her
down with a gag in her mouth.'

She paused, then in a fresh tone of voice said, 'Don't
make it difficult for me to go to Venice.'

A little smile, half a grin, came over his face, the grin
spread round the back of his head and reappeared round
the front again.

'How did you do that?' she asked.

'It's a trick of the light,' said the oaf.

He changed the subject: 'My divorce is going through,
the papers are being sent to my wife. If only it doesn't
bring her down on my head.'

'Then,' said Constance. 'Then you must keep a look out,
when you see her coming down you must step to one
side.'

The rain had stopped. He went out still naked and
barmy with sex, he brought back columbines and campions, new-mown hay, oak-tufts and honeysuckle, he put
oak sprays round her breasts, sticking in tufts of bluebells
and campion – straw in her hair. In her navel he placed
pink campions and in her pubic hair forget-me-nots.
Bird's-eye speedwell and woodruff.[60] She looked a mixture
of a flower bed and a scarecrow. The Oaf was well
pleased.

[60] How did it all stay on?

'That's you in all your glory,' he said. 'Lady Jane at her wedding with John Thomas.'

He hadn't finished. He stuck flowers in the hair of his own body, he wound a creeping-jenny round and around his penis, he stuck a single bell of hyacinth in his navel, he pushed a campion flower in his moustache and two up his nose.

At Buckingham Palace King George V and Queen Mary were just finishing dessert.

Constance was tiring of the floral arrangements.

'I really must go,' she said.

They started to dress.

'Say good-night to John Thomas,' he said, looking at his penis. 'He's safe in the arms of creeping-jenny!'

He was getting worse. He started talking as though to a wall, actually it was.

'Ay, I'll say nowt an' ha' done wi't. But tha mun dress thysen an' ga' back to a stately home.'

Oh dear, he was in the vernacular again. She never understood a word of vernac.

Halfway home Constance was met by a scarlet, puffing, perspiring Mrs Bolton, expending heat from every orifice. She was like a long-distance train arriving at Victoria.

'Sir Clifford thought you'd been killed by lightning, he was sending Field and Betts to find the body.'

They'd have found the body all right under another body fucking in the rain.

'How foolish of Clifford to make such a fuss,' said her ladyship.

'Oh, you know what men are,' said Mrs Bolton.

Yes, she knew what men were: she'd just left one.

'They like working themselves up,' said Mrs Bolton.

Constance knew that, she knew one who'd been working himself up her. She knew that Mrs Bolton knew, and Mrs Bolton knew that Constance knew that she knew. They both knew that each other knew. She could not pretend there was nothing between herself and the gamekeeper, only their clothes and they weren't on for long.

'Why, you're all right my lady! You've *only* been sheltering in the hut,' suggested Mrs Bolton. And pigs can fly!

SIXTEEN

THEY WENT ON into the house. Constance was furious with Clifford, furious with his pale face, his pale ears, furious with his prominent eyes, furious at his dead legs, furious at his prominent trousers, even his prominent brown shoes.

'I must say, I don't think you need send servants after me.'

'Very well, dear,' he replied, 'say it.'

She felt silly as she said, 'I don't think you need send servants after me.'

He berated her, he was an excellent barrator.

'Where have you been, woman?' he berated. 'What have you been up to?' He paused in his beration, then began berating again. 'It's hours since the rain stopped. Do you know what time it is?'

Why did he suddenly want to know the time? 'It's twenty past eight,' she said.

Seeing him so distressed, she felt a sudden qualm, she always kept a small qualm in her handbag, which she gave a quick feel.

'I've only been sheltering in the hut from the storm.' If you tell a lie, tell a big one.

'And look at your hair,' he berated. 'Look at yourself.'

She tried, she ran in circle after concentric circle trying to get a glimpse of herself; once or twice she saw her back

briefly, seeing 'the nicest arse of anybody'. That done, she
confessed to her barrator that she had run naked in the
rain, but omitted to mention forget-me-nots on the fanny.

He couldn't come to terms with what he'd heard. She
offered him reasonable terms but he refused.

'You must be mad!' he said.

'Why? What's wrong with a shower in the rain?!'

'Look! We have a perfectly good bath and shower here.
Do you have to wait until there's a thunderstorm before
you have a bath? My God, in the dry weather you'll go
lousy!'

His blood pressure was one sixty over one hundred and
ten. They waited till it came down to one hundred and
forty over ninety. To assist, Mrs Bolton threw a bucket of
water over him.

In a calm dripping voice he said, 'At least you'll be
lucky if you go off without a severe cold.'

'Oh, I haven't got a cold,' she replied.

Far from it, she had the 'hots'. Those magic words of
the gamekeeper kept going through her mind. 'Tha's got
nicest woman's arse of anybody.' But *how* did Mellors
know she had the nicest woman's arse of anybody? He had
told Berth Coutts the same thing! He'd only ever seen five
women's arses in his life; there must have been thousands
and thousands of women's arses out there better than Lady
Chatterley's. His comments on Lady Chatterley's arse were
completely unfounded; at judging arses he was a rank
amateur.

The time was nearing for her holiday in Venice. Hilda
arrived, she looked like a trainee Lesbian. She arrived in a
two-seater car with her suit-case strapped firmly behind.
(That *can't* be right!) Constance had arranged with Mellors
if everything promised well for their night together, she
would hang a green shawl out of the window; if it wasn't
she'd hang out a red one. She prayed he was not colour
blind.

'It will be so good', said Mrs Bolton, 'for your ladyship to have a change.'

Yes, Venice would be a great change from fucking naked in the woods during a thunderstorm.

'You don't mind looking after Sir Clifford while I'm away?'

Mrs Bolton didn't mind, he already owed her £8,000 playing pontoon; if this went on, soon Wragby Hall would be hers.

Constance confessed to Hilda she was carrying on with the gamekeeper.

'You'll regret it!' said Hilda.

'I shan't,' cried Constance.

No, she would never regret that twelve-inch prick.

'You'll get over him quite soon,' Hilda predicted.

Yes, she would get over him, he liked it like that.

'How old is this gamekeeper?' said Hilda.

'I don't know,' said Constance.

After their two days and nights of fucking he looked seventy.

'I would give up tonight's escapade,' said Hilda.

'No! I must stay with him tonight or I can't go to Venice.'

Hilda didn't know it but her sister was just one fuck away from Venice, then the holiday could start.

Hilda had the car ready for the assignation – the cuckolded husband thought they were driving to London for the boat train, like all good cuckolded husbands should – waving goodbye he shouted, 'Goodbye Hilda. Keep an eye on her.'

'I'll keep two,' said Hilda with lightning sharp wit. She could have said 'three' but a quick count of her optics would prove the lie.

Everybody waved. Constance looked back to see Sir Clifford being wheeled away by Mrs Bolton to pontoon and bankruptcy.

Constance wore her motoring goggles and disguising cap, even her own mother wouldn't have recognized her, primarily because she was dead. Because of Hilda's opposition, she would stand by her gamekeeper through thick and thin, indeed he was both, thick and thin. He admitted that when he was counting pheasants' eggs, after he got to twenty, his brain hurt.

They had stopped at the level-crossing to let the London train through, on board were the victorious London Irish Rugby Team. They had played a local village team from Garthby. By half time the Irish had amassed a total of 96 points to 3, therefore the Irish captain declared, so he and his team left, leaving the Garthby team to finish the game on their own. They went on to score 100 points and win.

Their car arrived at a footpath in the woods.

'Here we are,' said Constance.

Hilda looked around, indeed Constance was right. Here they were. She saw[61] a shadowy figure.

'Shadowy figure, who are you?' said Constance excitedly.

'I am', said shadowy figure, 'Oliver Mellors, gamekeeper to Lord Chatterley of Wragby Hall.'

So shadowy figure was him, what luck. Shadowy figure could have been anybody, it was anybody and he was called Oliver Mellors. They waited for Hilda to get out. But Hilda shut the door of the car and sat tight.

'This is my sister, who has shut the car door and is sitting tight. Won't you come and speak to her? Hilda, this is Mister Mellors.'

The gamekeeper lifted his hat.

'Is that it?' said Hilda. 'Can't the fellow talk?'

He mumbled some kind of reply but stopped when his brain hurt.

'Hilda, do come to the cottage,' pleaded Constance.

[61] Author's note.

The gamekeeper led the way.

'He knows these woods like the back of his hands,' said Constance.

Why then, thought Hilda, are we all struggling in the middle of a bramble thicket trying to escape?

Lacerated from head to foot, they eventually found the path. He went on ahead, they followed on foot. There was a fresh sweet scent in the air. It was his Anzora haircream. Nobody spoke. There was nothing to say, but any minute he might lift his hat yet again. What should have been a ten-minute walk took an hour.

'I took a wrong turning,' he said.

'No!' said Hilda. 'You took *every* wrong turning.'

Inside the cottage they sat around the fire. He seemed nervous of Hilda, he kept a distance from her, backing away from her against the wall.

'Would you like a drink?'

Yes! The girls would like Pol Roger's Champagne Brut Vintage 1921. He didn't 'ave that but had tea, cocoa or coffee. Would they like to eat? He had tripe and onions, pigs' trotters. Yes. He laid the food on the table.

''Elp yerselves,' he said. ''Elp yerselves, dybba waut f'r axin.'

'For God's sake, speak English, man,' shrilled Hilda. 'And while I'm on, what is this about you and my sister?'

'Yo maun ax'er.'

'For Christ's sake, speak *English*,' ranted Hilda.

'Women like you might 'appen a bin a good apple 'stead of a 'ansom clab.'

'Speak *English* you stupid bastard,' she yelled, put her coat on and left.

Good time for a fuck. He started to unlace his boots, by the time he had, Lady Chatterley was already naked, applying Vaseline.

It was a night of sensual passion in which she was a little startled and *almost* unwilling as this great steaming prick plunged up and down her like a sewerage station beam engine. The room was silent save for her gasps, his grunts, the twanging of the bed springs and the occasional cracking of the rheumatism in his knees. In their convulsions, every huge thrust caused her head to thud against the headboard, the sequence of noises went ooooh-ahhh doinggg-doinggg-crackle-crackled-thud! The passion consumed her through her bowels and breast. She thought she was dying, she got it wrong she wasn't dying. She meant fucked to death. In this short summer night she had learnt so much, for instance she'd never been fucked standing on her head before. 'It's like them Indian sculptures in the Ajantha Caves,' explained her tutor.

Came morning. They were both partially stuck to the bed and each other.

'Is it time to wake up?' she said.

He looked at the clock on the mantelpiece, the small hand was midway twix six and seven, the long hand on six. Why! 'That must be half past six,' he said. Her sister would be here at seven.

'My sister is very prompt,' she said.

Sure enough, her sister arrived promptly at twenty past eight. When Hilda saw Constance she was shocked, overnight she had lost a stone! This man was fucking her sister away.

'Thank God, you're not seeing him for some time,' said Hilda as they drove away.

SEVENTEEN

I N LONDON they stayed at White's Hotel. Sir Malcolm took Constance to the opera. He was modestly stout with stout thighs, she could see his dogged independence in his well-knit thighs. His strong, thick male legs were virile and alert; by all this it would appear her father was at the opera with no trousers on.

Madame Butterfly was singing, '*Spira sul mare e sulla.*' Constance woke up to the existence of legs. They became more important to her than a face, I mean a face couldn't get anywhere without legs. '*Terra un prima veril soffio giaconda*' sang Butterfly. How few people have live, alert legs like Nijinsky. Butterfly continued, '*Io sono la fanciulla!*' Those men in the stalls. Great puddingy thighs in black pudding cloth. '*Pie lieta del Giappone anzi del mondi!*' came Butterfly's soaring voice. Lean wooden-sticked legs. So the leg obsession continued. Butterfly was about to commit Hari-Kari. '*Tu, tu, piccolò Iddio,*' she sobbed. There were well-shaped legs without any meaning, the final curtain fell on the dying Cio-Cio-San. Constance came out humming Madame Butterfly's and Lieutenant Pinkerton's legs.

Paris. Constance was not happy in Paris. She was not happy again in Switzerland. She was equally again unhappy in the Tyrol. How she wished she was in the caves of Ajantha in India. Hilda and Constance 'did' Venice. From there came news via a letter from Mrs Bolton. Mellor's wife had returned; he had arrived home tired out from a day counting pheasants' eggs, to find her naked in bed, but he wasn't having any of it. Consequently she didn't get any of it. Sir Clifford had heard a rumour about him and Constance. He confronted him but Mellors, like a true Christian, said it was all lies.

Constance wished he had admitted it and said 'Yes, we want to get married and have a Thompson's ten-day Vaseline and Kama sutra holiday in the Ajantha Caves in Bombay.'

Back at Wragby Sir Clifford again confronted Mellors with the allegation saying he was a disreputable swine who walked about with his breeches' buttons undone. Mellors replied that Clifford had nothing to unbutton them for. Mellors was sacked on the spot, he was to leave the area or be shot.

GAMEKEEPER NAMED AS OTHER MAN

said the *Tevershall Times*. Indeed the gamekeeper had been having a lot of the other.

Mellors, the mean bastard, sent her a telegram that had 'to be paid by the recipient'. He was staying with his old landlady, Mrs Aida Grotts, No. 4 Terrible Street, Lewisham.

EIGHTEEN

CONSTANCE WAS confused. She did not know what to say or do. So she said and did nothing, which is exactly the same as not knowing what to say or do. First she told her father, 'I'm going to have a child.' He was unconscious for three minutes. A bucket of water brought him round.

'Whose child?' he asked.

'*Mine*, of course,' she said.

'Oh good!' he said. 'As long as it isn't anybody else's.'

She wrote Mellors asking him to meet her at Hartlands Hotel. Oh London. On arrival there she found a letter from him.

> I won't come around to your hotel, but will wait for you outside the Golden Cock[62] at 7.

They sat in the Golden Cock.

'My, you look well,' he said. 'Have you been away?'

She broke the news. 'I'm going to have a baby.'

He was unconscious for three minutes. Revived, he felt little flames run over his belly, a rare condition known as the shits.

He was silent then said, 'They used to say I had too much of a woman in me.'

---

[62] Was Lawrence serious?

The reverse applied, there'd been too much of him in a woman.

'You've got more than most men,' she said.

That he had.

She looked so lovely, warm and wistful, his bowels stirred towards her with a loud rumbling and gurgling.

'I suppose we can go to my room,' he said, feeling a glow in his trousers.

They walked to No. 4 Terrible Street. Up to his attic, by the time they'd reached the top she was undressed. Soon the people in the room below heard what they thought was a donkey-engine.

'Oh yes! yes!' she uttered in a sexual delirium. 'I'll leave Wragby and live with you.'

The rest of the night was a conveyor-belt of coitus. When morning came she told him, 'The baby's due in February.'

He was unconscious for three minutes.

Constance confided in her father.

'Where did his gamekeeper spring from?' he asked.

'Originally from a bush, he's very presentable.'

'He sounds like a gold-digger to me.'

'Oh, I've never heard that sound – and I've stood very close to him.'

'Think of how your stepmother would take it.'

Constance thought of how her stepmother would take it.

To have the baby Constance went to her family's home in Scotland. Mellors got a job on a farm as a labourer at thirty shillings all found. So far he hadn't found anything. Constance wrote to Clifford saying she was leaving him, what she left him was never revealed.

THE END

Discover more about our forthcoming books through Penguin's FREE newspaper...

Penguin
Quarterly

It's packed with:

- exciting features
- author interviews
- previews & reviews
- books from your favourite films & TV series
- exclusive competitions & much, much more...

Write off for your free copy today to:
Dept JC
Penguin Books Ltd
FREEPOST
West Drayton
Middlesex
UB7 0BR
NO STAMP REQUIRED

READ MORE IN PENGUIN

In every corner of the world, on every subject under the sun, Penguin represents quality and variety – the very best in publishing today.

For complete information about books available from Penguin – including Puffins, Penguin Classics and Arkana – and how to order them, write to us at the appropriate address below. Please note that for copyright reasons the selection of books varies from country to country.

In the United Kingdom: Please write to *Dept. JC, Penguin Books Ltd, FREEPOST, West Drayton, Middlesex UB7 OBR.*

If you have any difficulty in obtaining a title, please send your order with the correct money, plus ten per cent for postage and packaging, to *PO Box No. 11, West Drayton, Middlesex UB7 OBR*

In the United States: Please write to *Consumer Sales, Penguin USA, P.O. Box 999, Dept. 17109, Bergenfield, New Jersey 07621-0120.* VISA and MasterCard holders call 1-800-253-6476 to order all Penguin titles

In Canada: Please write to *Penguin Books Canada Ltd, 10 Alcorn Avenue, Suite 300, Toronto, Ontario M4V 3B2*

In Australia: Please write to *Penguin Books Australia Ltd, P.O. Box 257, Ringwood, Victoria 3134*

In New Zealand: Please write to *Penguin Books (NZ) Ltd, Private Bag 102902, North Shore Mail Centre, Auckland 10*

In India: Please write to *Penguin Books India Pvt Ltd, 706 Eros Apartments, 56 Nehru Place, New Delhi 110 019*

In the Netherlands: Please write to *Penguin Books Netherlands bv, Postbus 3507, NL-1001 AH Amsterdam*

In Germany: Please write to *Penguin Books Deutschland GmbH, Metzlerstrasse 26, 60594 Frankfurt am Main*

In Spain: Please write to *Penguin Books S. A., Bravo Murillo 19, 1° B, 28015 Madrid*

In Italy: Please write to *Penguin Italia s.r.l., Via Felice Casati 20, I–20124 Milano*

In France: Please write to *Penguin France S. A., 17 rue Lejeune, F–31000 Toulouse*

In Japan: Please write to *Penguin Books Japan, Ishikiribashi Building, 2–5–4, Suido, Bunkyo-ku, Tokyo 112*

In Greece: Please write to *Penguin Hellas Ltd, Dimocritou 3, GR–106 71 Athens*

In South Africa: Please write to *Longman Penguin Southern Africa (Pty) Ltd, Private Bag X08, Bertsham 2013*

BY THE SAME AUTHOR

A Selection

The Bible According to Spike Milligan

There have been many versions of the Old Testament over the centuries but never one quite like this. Spike Milligan has rewritten, in his own inimitable style, many of the best-known stories of the Old Testament, featuring characters like King (my brain hurts) Solomon, the great oaf of a giant Goliath and the well-known *Telegraph* crossword clue, Hushai the Archite. Believers and non-believers alike will enjoy this hilarious re-working, where the jokes, jests and jibes tumble over each other from Chapter One, Verse One until the end.

Adolf Hilter: My Part in His Downfall

Bathos, pathos, gales of drunken laughter, and insane military goonery explode in superlative Milliganese.

'Rommel?' 'Gunner Who?'

More Milligan military mania, but with a few Desert Rats thrown in for good measure!

Mussolini: His Part in My Downfall

Britannia rules the waves, but sometimes she waives the rules, and Spike is set to libertate - *gasp* – Italy.

Where Have All the Bullets Gone?

In response to pressing demands from the Inland Revenue, the fifth volume of Mr Milligan's inimicable war memoirs.

Goodbye Soldier

'There is no one living and, with the exception of Groucho Marx, no one dead, to match him at his best' – *Observer*

Peace Work

It's 1946 and Spike, newly demobbed, goes on tour all over Britain and parts of Europe. Then he teams up with Harry Secombe, Michael Bentine and Peter Sellers. They became 'The Goons'. The rest is history.